B.O.S.S.
Break Out Silent Soldier

JODY PAAR

Copyright © 2018 by Jody Paar

B.O.S.S. Break Out Silent Soldier

All rights reserved. No part of this publication may be reproduced, distributed, or transmitted in any form or by any means, including photocopying, recording, or other electronic or mechanical methods, without the prior written permission of the publisher, except in the case of brief quotations embodied in critical reviews and certain other noncommercial uses permitted by copyright law. For permission requests, write to the publisher, addressed "Attention: Permissions Coordinator," at info@beyondpublishing.net

Quantity sales special discounts are available on quantity purchases by corporations, associations, and others. For details, contact the publisher at the address above.

Orders by U.S. trade bookstores and wholesalers. Email info@BeyondPublishing.net

The Beyond Publishing Speakers Bureau can bring authors to your live event. For more information or to book an event contact the Beyond Publishing Speakers Bureau speak@BeyondPublishing.net

The Author can be reached directly BeyondPublishing.net/AuthorJodyPaar

Manufactured and printed in the United States of America distributed globally by BeyondPublishing.net

BEYOND
PUBLISHING

New York | Los Angeles | London | Sydney

10 9 8 7 6 5 4 3 2 1   978-1-947256-43-9

DEDICATION

I dedicate this book to my husband Jim Paar, the man who saw the beauty instead of the pain, who slowly put all the broken pieces back together and showed me what true love was, who supports and loves me like no other, and who pushed me to be the person I never knew I was. I love you more.

EPIGRAPH

"Even ***though I walk through the valley of the shadow of death,*** I will fear no evil, for you are with me; your rod and your staff, they comfort me" (Psalm 23:4).

ACKNOWLEDGMENTS

First and foremost, thank you, God, for breaking off all my chains, for loving me so much when I didn't love myself, for protecting me so many times I should have been dead. I give God all the glory for this book.

Jim Paar (my husband) Thank you for EVERYTHING! You are my soul mate and rock in life. Words can't begin to express the gratitude I have for you always being there for me. I couldn't have done this without you. Teddy and Tuttles, my sweet fur babies, Mommy loves you so much!

Thank you, Mom (Peggy Thomas) for always believing more for me and always sticking beside me. I love you, Mom.

Thank you, Joe Thomas, my daddy in heaven, for always teaching me to be a better person. I love and miss you, Daddy.

I want to thank my sister Melinda Ladner for teaching me at a young age how to be glamourous. I love you, Sis.

Thanks to my other sister Melissa Comeaux for being there for me in my darkest hour to my brightest moment. I love you, Sissy.

Thanks to the best in-laws anyone could ask for--Joe and Joan Paar. Thank you for believing in me. I love you, Mom and Dad.

Mary Thomas (my Mawmaw in heaven,) thank you for giving

me my stubbornness. I love you, Mawmaw. I miss you.

Thank you, June Moore (my other grandma in heaven) for teaching me the values of life. I love you, Grandma June. I miss you.

I want to thank Pete Moore (my grandpa in heaven) for teaching me to be tough and have thick skin. I love and miss you.

Thank you for making my life sweeter, Nick and Sam Keis, my stepson and his wife and my grandson Gavin Keis. I love you.

I want to give a huge thank you to the rest of my extended family: my nieces, nephews, brother in-laws, and sister in-law. Thank you for all the love and support. I love you all.

Thank you, Michael Butler with Beyond Publishing, for publishing my book and believing in me.

I want to thank Sherrie Clark with Storehouse Media Group. Thank you for the amazing editing, teaching, and talks. Your team is amazing!

Thank you, Paar Media Group, for all artwork on my website and book. I am so thankful you brought my vision to life for the cover. You are the best!

I want to thank Bruce Hill for coaching me to be a fierce speaker.

Forbes Riley, thank you for coaching me, pushing me out of my comfort zone, and empowering me to be the woman I am today. I would not be where I am without you. I love you, Forbes.

To my best friend Amanda Griffin, thank you for being my best friend throughout this whole process, for staying on the phone with me through breakdowns and breakthroughs, for pushing me when I wanted to give up so many times. Words can't express how grateful I am for you walking beside me through it all. Even when we were miles apart, you made a way to be there for me. I love you!

To my best friends, Debra Fortson, Heather Nowlin, Lora Fowler, Tammy Myers, Tereasa Richardson, and Tiffanie Carlson, thank you for supporting and believing in me. I love you all so much.

To Vickie Robinson and Judy Worley, thank you for giving me shelter when I had nowhere to go and feeding me when I was hungry. I love you.

I want to thank the Knight family for being the biggest supporters of me from the very beginning. Love this little family.

Kristina Marriot, thank you for pushing me for the deliverance I needed to break the chains and be set free. You helped me do that! I love you.

Thanks to the Grant Cardone family for having the 10X event that changed my life.

I want to thank the ones who hurt me in friendship, relationships, careers, and life. You know who you are.

Thank you to every single person who believed in me!

Thanks to every person who reads this book. Thank you from the bottom of my heart for the love and support.

And I want to thank every victim of any kind of abuse. I acknowledge you; I believe you, and you are not alone.

CONTENTS

Introduction   9

Chapter ONE: Stubborn Li'l Princess   10

Chapter TWO: Was I Born Stupid?   20

Chapter THREE: The Rebellious Teenager   28

Chapter FOUR: Running into Danger   40

Chapter FIVE: Running Scared   73

Chapter SIX: Running into Robbie   81

Chapter SEVEN: Running into Drugs   108

Chapter EIGHT: Fear and Paybacks   124

About the Author: JODY PAAR   146

INTRODUCTION

When I first came up with the name of this book, it was *B.O.S.S.: Break out Silent Sisters,* but I realized both females and males are silent soldiers. I wrote this book for the people who are silenced and still suffering. Past experiences falling on people and making them so hard, no one can break them down.

How does one deal with this? How does one escape the invisible prison bars? When the wolf comes around, how does one not become a scared sheep and tremble in fear?

In this three-book series I will take you on the journey of my life that will answer each of these questions. I will go deep into detail of what I have been through: the good, the bad, and the very ugly. I will go through how God broke chains and set this prisoner free.

This is a true story, but, of course, I did change some of the names and details to protect the people in my life. The world has nourished perversion, causing it to be more prevalent. If we all keep silent, then it only gets fed more. I am no longer hiding in fear.

Now is the time for all Silent Soldiers to break free.

I felt hopeless, I felt worthless, but that was only lies. I pray my story gives you hope and that you realize if I can change my life around, you can too.

The only difference between bitter and better is one letter, and that's the letter "i."

Chapter One

STUBBORN LI'L PRINCESS

Once upon a time a star was born. However, this star felt dim and it took many years before she would shine.

I grew up in a small town and was very sheltered from the real world. My world consisted of home, church, school, grandparents – and those were pretty much the only places I went. I was the child who thought that every home was happy and safe. I was the baby of the family, and let's just say it…spoiled! My middle sister really spoiled me, so it is her fault, not mine.

My dad would always take my sister hunting and I really wanted to go too. When I was six years old, I approached my daddy resting in his recliner, sound asleep after a long day at work. I screamed at the top of my lungs, "Daddy, you take Melissa all the time. When is it my turn?"

He jumped like his pants were on fire. After realizing everything was okay, he said, "Okay you can go with me Saturday morning." I squealed with excitement. He put a serious look on his face as he gave me his agenda. "We'll leave at 6:00 a.m."

My eyes opened wide from shock. "What? Dad, 6:00 is so early."

He raised his left eyebrow. "Do you want to go or not?"

I thought about the fun I would have with my daddy and smiled. "Yes, Daddy! Yes!" I took my little booty down the hallway to announce to my sister, "I'm going hunting with Daddy, and you're not." Then I turned on my heel and pranced out the door.

Melissa rolled her eyes. "Of course, you are."

By 6:00 that next morning, I was up and dressed to go hunting in orange pants with black rain boots, my sister's orange knit hat, and my sister's camouflage jacket that swallowed me and fit more like a dress. No worries, I was determined to wear it anyway. Of course, I still had to keep the diva in my attire, so I wore fuzzy, pink gloves, proving that one can be fashionable when hunting.

On the way we stopped at this little store. As we pulled into the parking lot, there were several trucks covered with mud, carrying wooden dog boxes containing excited and barking hound dogs. When we walked inside the store, several men were standing and drinking hot chocolate or coffee, chomping on biscuits, and telling their stories about the one that got away. All of them were dressed in orange and camouflage and looked like trees so they could blend in with the real trees. Their fashion was hideous.

My daddy got me the biggest honey bun I had ever seen. *This hunting thing is fun,* I thought. We left the store and drove into the woods that seemed to be in the middle of nowhere. When we got to the hunting spot, Daddy told me I had two options. First, I could get up in the tree stand with him, but I would have to be quiet. Second, I could sit in the truck, watch the animals, and talk to the other hunters on the CB radio.

Anyone who knows me knows I've always liked to talk – even at that young age – so sit in the truck it was. I was Baby Bear on the radio, so I talked to the other hunters and ate my honey bun. Hunting didn't seem so bad at all.

Then suddenly, all of these rabbits came out to play. They were so cute. It was kind of like a movie, entertaining as I watched all of the animals play. My daddy was stuck up in that tree stand which was so boring. *I would much rather sit in the truck*, I thought.

A long time went by and a cute little deer came out. This was around the time Bambi was popular, and I thought, *Wow! It's Bambi!* Then the mommy deer came out to eat some grass too. I was just loving that I came hunting with Daddy.

Then, the BIGGEST deer I have ever seen in my life joined the others. This deer had huge antlers and stood tall, just like Bambi's daddy did in the movie. I noticed my dad start to move. I wondered what he was doing. He grabbed his huge gun.

Oh no! He is going to shoot Bambi's daddy! HONK! HONK! HONK! RUN DEER RUN! My daddy's gonna kill you!

Thank God, all the deer scattered like crazy, and my daddy missed. Man, that was close. It was then that Daddy climbed down out of his deer stand, his body tensed up, rushing toward me. He opened the door, his face as red as could be. "Why did you do that?"

"Because you were going to kill Bambi's daddy," I screamed back. My little heart was about to burst out of my chest. I was so angry at my daddy. I saw those mean hunters in the movie kill Bambi's daddy, and I thought my daddy was one of them. I may have been little, but I was a firecracker, standing my ground to protect Bambi's daddy.

We rode in silence the whole way home. When I tried to talk to him, there was no reply. At home he opened the door and sat me down while I cried. When I got angry, I cried.

"Take her shopping," he told my mom. "She will never hunt with me again."

And I didn't.

You Left Me!

I grew up in a Christian home, and I was in church every Sunday morning and night and Wednesday nights too. One time my mom thought my dad took me home after church, and my dad thought I rode home with Mom, but they both had left me at church.

I think this was the first little bit of fear I felt as a child. I chased the car down the hill waving my hands and screaming, but Mom didn't see me. I sat on the side of the road, crying until Mr. Larry and Mrs. Janice picked me up and hugged me.

"We'll take you home, sweetheart," they said.

The church was a good 20 minutes from our house. Janice and Larry had a daughter Shelly, who was one of my good friends, and I played at her house a lot. Mr. Larry also hunted with my daddy and they were good friends. I knew I would be safe going with them. As I sat in the backseat looking out the window, my lip stuck out as I pouted, and tears ran down my face. I couldn't believe they left me.

When we pulled up, I saw Daddy, arms flinging and face scowling like an angry dog. I am sure my parents were arguing about who was supposed to take me home. Momma was behind the wheel, either just pulling up or leaving to come get me. I saw the look soften on Daddy's face when that red car pulled into the driveway.

My mom jumped out of the car, a huge smile of relief on her face. I ran as fast as my little legs would take me and jumped into her arms. Then as I pulled my head back to look her in the eyes, the little diva came out in me again. With my big lip poked out as far as it would go I snapped, "You left me."

"I am so sorry," Momma said, hugging me tight. My daddy took a deep breath and slowly walked over to thank Larry and Janice for getting me safely home. With a huge grin under his mustache Larry replied. "No problem at all."

You can bet my lip stayed poked out all night long. With my little forehead wrinkled up I whispered for the twentieth time, "I can't believe BOTH of you left me."

What's That Smell?

I used to visit my daddy's parents a lot. School was out, and it was time to enjoy the sunshine. In this small little house lived my Mawmaw, Pawpaw, and my great-grandma, Kitty Mouse. I don't know why they called her Kitty Mouse, because she was more of a mountain lion. She might have been small, but she was fierce!

As a child, I noticed that Mawmaw and Pawpaw didn't love on each other that much. She usually stood, arms crossed with a stare at him that should have melted him right then and there. He stood, tall chest poked out, voice carrying all through the house. He would spew at her and she spewed right back at him.

She was very tough, and I feel that is where some of my strength comes from. When we went to use the bathroom, Mawmaw left us four squares of tissue paper on the back of the toilet. One day while she was in the kitchen frying bacon for breakfast, I asked, "Mawmaw, are we poor?"

She turned around to look at me. "Why, sweetie?"

"Because we don't have a whole roll of toilet paper here."

She turned back around and started turning the bacon over. "Children don't know how to handle a whole roll. Four sheets are plenty for a child."

Hmm, I thought, *I guess the bigger the booty the more toilet paper you need.* To this day I always wonder if I am using too much toilet paper.

We would load up in her big old station wagon to head down to Kmart. Her station wagon was huge and had seats that sat sideways. We always brought her little dogs with us too. The dogs and the kids rolled around the back of the big station wagon.

My mouth watered, and my tummy growled with excitement when we went to eat at Pawpaw's restaurant. Driving down the dirt road, we would see on both sides the most beautiful horses roaming in the open fields. At the end of the road was *The Crazy Horse Saloon,* and *The Chaparral.* I always thought Pawpaw was rich because he owned all this land and two buildings around which were always packed with cars or motorcycles. I wasn't allowed in the building with the crazy horse on it. We always went to The Chaparral, where the crispy French fries would melt in your mouth. I loved our trips to where Pawpaw worked, to eat and to see the horses.

I loved to ride Pawpaw's horses, but they would always stand up on two legs when I rode them. It was like a rocking horse on steroids. The horse would jerk and buck and that's usually when I went flying through the air. One time when I landed it was squishy and smelly! "Ewwww," I screamed. "I am not getting on another horse," I announced, stomping out of the field.

The corners of Pawpaw's mouth curled up as I approached him. "They can sense your fear, princess."

With my arms crossed and tapping my foot I replied, "Well, princesses and poop don't mix, Pawpaw!" Pawpaw found another way for me to love horses. I was the first and best horse caller. I made this high-pitched horse call and they all came running. I am not sure what I was saying in horse language. It must have been *dinner's ready.*

We made many trips to the bars, but I will never forget the last trip I took. Mawmaw sent me out to the car while she talked to Pawpaw after we had dinner. I, of course, didn't go to the car; I went to see the horses. As I was walking to the field, all the horses were nowhere to be seen. I then heard this noise as if one of the horses was hurt. It was a loud moaning noise. I wanted to get closer to see if one of the horses had fallen.

It was then I saw a man's booty bouncing up and down on this woman. *He is hurting her.* I screamed as loud as I could, "Get off her!" They both jumped up like hot grease in a frying pan. Reaching for clothes the guy yelled at me to "come here."

"NO!" I screamed, "I am telling my Mawmaw!" Arms flinging and little legs moving as fast as they could, I ran into the forbidden building with the crazy horse on it. As I walked inside I couldn't see much for the thick layer of smoke. *It stinks in here.* People were smiling at me, some with teeth, some without. I wrinkled up my little nose at them smiling at me.

I spotted Mawmaw sitting at the bar smoking on a cigarette and tapping her foot. Pawpaw got loud, Mawmaw got louder. I tugged on Mawmaw's shirt. She continued her deep discussion with Pawpaw. They were both ignoring me. "I SAW NAKED PEOPLE!" I screamed. The burning ember from Mawmaw's cigarette fell in her lap. She jumped up to brush it off.

"WHAT?" she asked. With my fists balled up and arms at my side, I stood up on my toes. "I saw a man's booty in the field; he was on a woman and she was moaning like a hurt horse."

Mawmaw's eyes widened and then turned dark as she turned to Pawpaw with horror on her face. She grabbed my hand and shook her finger as she spoke in Pawpaw's ear. Her eyes were locked with mine as she asked, "Where?" I walked out of that smoke-filled bar like a proud peacock ready to show my Mawmaw what I saw.

As we got closer to the field no one was there. *What?* I was confused. My head went from side to side. I stood up on my tippy toes. *Where did they go?* I turned with eyes of disappointment. "They are not here."

"What did they look like?" Mawmaw's eyes narrowed in on mine.

"Naked," I replied. Her frown softened, and the corners of her mouth curled up a little trying not to laugh.

"Well, I don't see any naked people now."

"Me either." Mawmaw grabbed my hand we walked back to the car. "We will get our food to go from now on." Mawmaw buckled my seatbelt. That was the last trip to see Pawpaw at his bars.

"I wonder what we will hear on the scanner tonight," I said in excitement, jumping up and down on the bed.

"Stop jumping on the bed and come lay beside me, child." Mawmaw had on her big robe and I snuggled in the bed beside her. I always loved this time, waiting up for Pawpaw and listening to the police scanner. "The bird that stays up all night alert is the owl," Mawmaw grinned.

"We are owls," I grinned back.

"Yes, we are; night owls."

My little eyes fought staying open and they slowly closed like curtains on a window. I would stay up as late as I could, but always fell asleep before Pawpaw came home. I always knew when Pawpaw was home because he stunk. I never knew what alcohol was as a little girl. Like I said, I was very sheltered. Pawpaw, however, always wore this horrible cologne. He must have bathed in it because it seeped out of his breath and pores and filled the whole room with that smell. It reminded me of the gas smell when you pump too much, and it overflows. Like a nasty chemical that is strong. I always thought he needed to switch to Old Spice; it smelled much better.

When he came home Mawmaw always told me to stay in the bedroom. As usual, I didn't listen and snuck down the hallway. Pawpaw, swaying from side to side with a red face, stood at the kitchen sink yelling and cursing. His fist would slam down and my little body would shake as I eavesdropped on them. Pawpaw raised his fist and swung around in a circle missing Mawmaw. The second time he tried his head was greeted with a skillet full of eggs.

"Think twice, old drunk man," she said, as she dropped the skillet on the floor with the scattered scrambled eggs. I boogied my booty back down the hall and jumped into bed. Mawmaw was a super hero! I bet that is where I get my boldness from too.

It took years before I knew the monster my Pawpaw was. He was a broken man addicted to women and alcohol. He was very abusive and hateful. My daddy always prayed for him, and I am thankful that he accepted Jesus on his deathbed. He now walks the streets of gold with my dad. It is never too late to change your life and put that pain under the blood of Jesus. Jesus doesn't care about your past but wants to give you freedom in your future.

We must remember that fear can be instilled in us as a child, and we carry that into adulthood. Give God your life, and just as you blow ashes into the air your fear too will disappear.

Chapter Two

WAS I BORN STUPID?

The second thing about my childhood that reminds me of fear was a big one. It's the one word that still sends shivers down my spine: the "S" word – School!

As a small child in kindergarten through fourth grade, school wasn't that bad. Denise, who had long pretty hair, was piling pine straw into four squares. I walked over, my eyebrows raised, and forehead wrinkled up. "What cha doing?"

She lifted her head and looked at me, her face lit up like a light bulb. "I am building a house for my pound puppies."

"Oh!" My mouth flew open and I walked closer to get a better look. "I will build a house too for my pound puppies." That cute little girl and I are still friends to this day. In the beginning school was fun! Junior high was a little harder, but I made a C, D, or F on my report card. (And I was a master at changing an F to an A before my parents saw it.)

When I turned 16 is when I really started to notice that something was different about my learning. *Why am I not learning as quickly as all the other students?* While other students focused on the teachers, I focused on the room. *I wonder where Jessica got those Keds from?*

They are so cute. My eyes shot across to the other side of the room, widening with excitement. Anthony leaned over almost knocking over his desk to slide a piece of paper to Amanda. I scanned the room some more and noticed that Jerry was sleeping and slobbering all over his desk… EWW!

"Ms. Thomas!" My heart nearly jumped out of my chest as I turned and saw this grey-haired woman, along with the whole class, staring at me.

"Yes," I answered, heart racing.

Her eyebrows narrowed, her eyes seeming to penetrate my skull. "What is the answer?"

Ummm. I had to think fast. I had no idea what she had been talking about. "Can you repeat the question?" I wanted to disappear under my desk.

With her face turning as red as the shirt on the kid across the room, she asked, "How many children did Thomas Jefferson have?"

"Oh! That's easy," I said, with diva attitude. "A lot!" The whole classroom burst into laughter, except for the angry woman who was still sending lasers into me.

"I will see you after class, Ms. Thomas," she snapped.

I sat straight up in my desk. "Did I win a prize?"

"Not exactly, young lady," she said as she turned on her heels to face the chalkboard.

I sat in this boring room when I should have been watching "Fraggle Rock" and eating chicken nuggets after school. A guy with greasy hair sat across from me, wearing a black leather jacket and big black boots with silver chains on them. "What did you do to end up in here?" he asked, while chewing on the end of a pen?

He is going to have black ink all over him I thought. "I don't know. I guess being stupid in class." My eyes lowered in shame. "What about you?" I asked in curiosity.

Deep dimples appeared as he looked at me. "I peed on a plant."

"Oh. I bet that's good for the soil," I winked.

"My name is Justin." He reached his hand out.

"NO TALKING" came from the front of the room where a tall, baldheaded skinny man sat behind his paper.

Quietly I whispered, "I am Jody."

I finally had it and refused to study anymore. *Why study? It isn't like I will remember it.* I began to hang out in detention after school so I could see Justin. Bad boys bring trouble. "Have you ever skipped school?" Those dimples were talking to me. I was putting on lip gloss and shook my head from side to side. His hand touched my knee and shivers of excitement went through me. As his beautiful blue eyes looked deep into mine he replied, "You should."

High school was so hard, and I seriously dreaded it. My blonde bombshell friend and I sat on the bleachers having our period for the third time in a month – or at least that's what we told our gym teacher. I started to tap my lip in deep thought. "So, have you ever thought of skipping school?"

AJ almost choked on her gum and her eyes widened. "No," she leaned in closer, "but I have always wanted to." We slid down the bleachers closer to the back door. Ready. *One, two, three*, and we opened the door to sunlight and ran towards AJ's car.

"Let's ride by Justin's house to see if he's home," I winked at AJ.

As we turned onto Justin's dirt road we noticed huge mud puddles. AJ turned to me, her hands white-knuckled on the steering wheel. "Think we can make it?"

"Sure!" I jumped up and down and cranked up the radio. Her little car took off like a bullet, full speed ahead. We reached the puddle and water splashed everywhere. "Keep going," I yelled, but that wasn't happening. The wheels were turning but we were stuck. AJ's face went blank. "My mom is going to kill me."

I looked at her in pure guilt. "We will call my mom." As I opened the door, mud was everywhere. I stuck my foot down and sank all the way up to my thighs.

"Jody!" AJ was also covered in mud.

"I heard it's good for your skin," I laughed. "We have to walk to my aunt's house, AJ. I know where she leaves the key." We hosed off outside and snuck in the empty house to call my mom. "Mom, I am all muddy and need you to come get me at Aunt Cindy's."

"Aren't you supposed to be in school?" she asked.

"Well, kind of..."

My mom was and is still my best friend. I saw the Oldsmobile turn up the driveway, dust flying behind it. "Are we going to die?" AJ's face was white as a ghost.

"If that was my dad, yes. My mom is cool."

Cool isn't what my mom was at all. "Jody! What were you thinking?" I lowered my head and balled my body up in the fetal position. "I am going to have to tell your dad."

"NO!" I screamed. "Please don't tell him." I sat straight up. "I promise I won't do this again."

The corners of her mouth curled up. "Ok, but don't do this again."

When Justin heard about our escapade, he burst out laughing. "You amateur."

"Shut up!" I giggled back.

My parents made me go to school, and I hated it. I would sit there, the teacher sounding like Charlie Brown. Blah Blah Blah! I don't mean that to be funny – I really had no idea what she was talking about in algebra.

Some days I just slept. Mrs. Davis had this ruler, and she would pop my desk and say, "Wake up, Miss Jody." That was my history class, and I always wondered that since those people were dead, why did I have to learn about them? It was just another excuse, I told myself to feel better.

Other students comprehended what she said, but not me. I sat in the bathroom stall for hours reading the walls (before cell phones), which was entertaining. Some days I cried; other days I just sat still, but inside I felt so stupid. How was it everyone else understood the lessons, but I didn't?

I did love hanging out with the cheerleaders. That is what I really wanted to be, but you had to have good grades to do that. I knew I would rather be home than at school since nothing was working in my favor. Those negative thoughts got a hold of me, and it was downhill from there.

Before I close the chapter on how bad school was, I will say that choir was not bad. I loved Mrs. Jones so much. She was the piano player, and she told me how special I was. I never thought I was. She believed in me, and I never thought that she thought I was stupid. One time, she wanted me to sing a solo. I had such stage fright and told her there was no way. She told me I was a star, and everyone would love me.

I got to choose the song, and it ended up being the Oscar Meyer Wiener Song. How can you mess up that solo? As I walked out on the stage, my legs were shaking beneath me, and my heart was about to burst out of my chest. All the blank faces were staring at me, and Mom was holding this huge video camera as the red blinking light reminded me it was recording.

I walked up to the mic and wrapped my sweating hands around it. I begin to sing, "Oh I wish I was an Oscar Meyer Weiner." I sang louder. "That is what I truly want to be. 'Cause if I was an Oscar Meyer Weiner, everyone would be in love with me."

The crowd cheered so loudly, and I will never forget that beautiful choir teacher smiling at me. She pushed me because she believed in me. So, although I felt stupid in every class, I knew I could sing. We all loved Mrs. Jones, but I think I loved her a little more than the other students, because she inspired me, and I knew she believed in me.

Another part of childhood where I felt different from others was becoming a woman. It took forever for me to have "that time." I was so mad because all my friends did, and I didn't. I don't know what the heck I was thinking.

When the "aunt" I had heard so much about came along, she was fierce! I had the worst cramps ever. I had to go to an OB-GYN to see what was wrong. This was the first time a man was going to see my vagina. I told my mom no way is he going there. She held my hand and said, "This is part of being a woman."

The doctor seemed kind when he came in and greeted us. I noticed he had a lot of tools with him. I asked, "What the heck is that, and where are you sticking it?" It was so cold and hurt bad but not near the pain I would feel in the future. My doctor said I had something called endometriosis. That is basically when the scar tissue around your ovaries sets you on fire. It makes for the worst cramps ever.

At that point, I took back my plea to be a woman and told God I didn't want this "aunt" to visit anymore. The cramps only got worse, and my doctor told me I had to have laser surgery. I was in the hospital for a while and out of school for a month during my sophomore year. This girl who already felt stupid was at that point one month behind everyone else in class.

I felt that I couldn't even do well when I was there, and now, being a month behind, I was paralyzed with fear. I ended up dropping out of school. Funny how your mind can destroy your hopes and dreams.

I was determined to get my GED. It took me only a short time, so I realized I must not be that stupid. I was so nervous the first day I walked into class for my GED. I met the nicest guy there. I told him I was stupid, and he told me "No, you are a star." He was foreign and told me that if he could learn English, I could master the GED.

Although I did get my GED, the demon in my mind still said I wasn't smart. Not walking with my class at graduation ripped my heart out. That, by far, really took a toll on my life. I had the same dream for years: I walked under the bleachers, white and blue school colors everywhere. Familiar faces smiling and taking pictures with their proud parents. "Time to line up," someone would yell, and all my classmates would form a single line. I went to join them when a huge spotlight turned on me and a tall, pointed dunce cap sat on my head. All the students turned, pointed, and laughed.

I sat straight up in the bed with my heart racing. It was just a nightmare. I wanted so badly to attend my 10-year class reunion. "Are you stupid?" Antonio asked. (You will learn more about him in Series Two.)

"No!" Arms crossed, I glared at him.

"All those classmates are successful, you are a nobody," he said.

"Why would you go embarrass yourself like that?" I lowered my head as tears rolled down my face. I felt like he was right. *I am a dropout, not a graduate.*

Chapter Three

THE REBELLIOUS TEENAGER

The first time I ran away I was very young, maybe six. I packed up my Strawberry Shortcake backpack and took off. I was mad about not getting my way. I told Mom I was going to run away, and she said okay. So off I went. I went into the woods and was going to see how long it took them to find me.

I waited…and waited…and waited, but no one came. I saw my daddy come home from work and still no one came looking for me. It began to get dark, and I started to get scared, so I picked up my backpack, mad as a hornet. I was crying so hard and walked into that house ready for war. My mom had this huge smile on her face, and my sisters were laughing.

"No one loves me," I shouted.

No response.

"No one came to look for me," I added, with huge teardrops falling from my eyes.

My mom, with the biggest smile on her face, said, "Well, sweetie, next time you run away, make sure we can't see you through the woods."

My daddy was very strict, but he had a kind heart. Let's be honest – he had three daughters, and he stood tall, like a mountain man. Boys were always scared to date us, and rightfully so. My daddy protected us and made sure we were safe. A guy could only date us if he came over the night before and met my dad first. The guy had to sit with my dad and watch a movie and "talk" before he could take us on a date.

One guy, named Justin – yes, the same one from detention – came over. I was just drawn to him like a moth to a flame. I was excited he could finally take me out. We had been friends for a year and he finally asked me for a date. He came over and was watching TV. He had on this blue bandanna.

My sister Melissa giggled and said, "Ummm, I wouldn't wear that bandanna on your head to meet my dad."

Justin laughed. He wasn't scared, but he should have been. My sister also told him he had better shake our dad's hand when he came in. Justin leaned over and told me, "I don't shake hands."

"With those dimples you don't have to." I was a smitten kitten.

My daddy loved to hunt in the woods behind our house. He had just skinned a deer and was coming inside to wash his hands. Mom jumped up to grab the door.

Dad walked in, and my first thought was, *Oh, Justin, why did you have to keep the bandanna on your head?* My daddy came in and, with his bloody hand, took that bandanna right off, causing blood to drip down Justin's head. Justin's face turned white and his eyes widened.

My sister Melissa giggled again and said, "Told ya so," as she skipped into the kitchen. After that, Justin jumped out of his seat to shake my daddy's hands, but Daddy said he had to wash them first. Justin never wore a bandanna to the house again.

My dad visited with our dates. Often, he did this while cleaning his guns. Talk about being an embarrassed teenage girl. So, when I say that guys feared my dad, you can understand why. He always wrote down their tag number, and the make and model of their trucks. He told them to have his daughters home at twelve, no later. Justin and I were in love and he even gave me a little pink diamond promise ring. I was so in love.

Justin always followed these rules, except one time. We were all mudding and got stuck. I knew I had to be home at twelve, and it was 12:10. This was before cell phone days, so I had my friend take me to a pay phone. With each ring, my heart raced faster. *Please mom answer.* If Dad answered my life was over. When she picked up, I whispered, "Hello? Mom, it's me. I'm at a pay phone… Mom, we are stuck in the mud. Please, please, don't wake Daddy."

"I won't, sweetheart. Hurry home when you can." My mom knew I could be trusted and that I was not only a virgin, but also that I didn't drink. I was a good kid. She was also half awake.

We pulled up to the house with the porch light on. No other lights in the house were on and I breathed a sigh of relief. Hand in hand, Justin and I walked to the door. As I started to grab the doorknob, the door opened and there stood my dad, arms crossed, standing tall like a mountain. "Go to bed," he said to me while not taking his eye off of Justin.

Justin, scared, shuffled from one foot to the other, his eyebrows raised in concern. He looked down at me. "Goodnight."

Daddy's chest puffed out as he continued looking at Justin. "Not good for you."

I looked down, I was so embarrassed. Then I got a bit angry. *Why was he treating me like a little girl?* "I don't need you to protect me!" I screamed. Little did I know how much I would need my dad to protect me. My future self was about to learn that hard lesson.

*****

"I just don't think this is going to work out." Justin took my hand in his. "Jody, I just think you're too immature for me."

"What?" I jumped back, pulling my hand from his.

"AJ and I…" His eyes begin to look around the truck.

"WHAT, JUSTIN?" Tears began to pour out of my eyes.

"It just kinda happened." His eyes shut.

"You slept with her?" My heart was racing, and I couldn't concentrate. "She is my best friend."

"I know." Head still lowered, he grabbed my hand. "I need this back." I jerked my hand back.

"You gave me this ring."

"I know, but we are no longer together so it is mine now."

"Fine," I said, as I threw the ring and it bounced off his forehead. I got out of the truck and slammed the door as hard as I could.

I walked in the door crying. My dad was in his recliner reading the newspaper. His paper lowered. "Why are you crying, Jody?"

"Justin took my ring," I cried.

My dad took off out of the house like a rocket. He jumped in his truck and was gone.

"Oh no!" I screamed running into my sister's room. "Daddy is going to kill Justin."

"Good," Melissa smirked back. "I didn't like that little punk anyway."

Dad pulled up in his truck about fifteen minutes later. He walked in the house and placed the little ring in my hand. "I didn't kill him, but that boy better never walk in my door again."

"Thank you, Daddy." I wrapped my arms around his body.

"You're welcome." He kissed the top of my head.

The next day was Saturday. I sat on the bar stool in the kitchen as mom was making us sandwiches. "Mom." I kicked my feet nervously under the bar.

"Yes?" She turned to me.

"Do you think I should have slept with Justin? We would still be together."

"Jody." She walked over to me, placed her hands on my shoulders and looked at me – eyeball to eyeball. "If a man really loves you, he will wait for you. This is a gift you can't get back. Save it for the one you marry who you know will never leave you. I smiled in agreement with my mom.

I wasn't a bad teenager. I didn't drink, didn't want to drink, but my friends sure did. One time, my friends wanted to go cow tipping, and I went along for the ride. If you don't know what that is, you go into the fields, and once the cows go to sleep, you push them and tip them over. I never really understood the purpose of cow tipping, so I stayed in the car while they went in those fields. I think you had to be drunk to enjoy it. I felt bad for the cows. I sure don't want anyone to mess with me when I sleep. I loved it when some cows were not asleep and took off chasing them. Now that is funny to watch.

Another time when I went out with my friends, we took this girl named Leann home. She was so drunk that she got stuck as she tried to sneak back in her window. We pushed and pushed on her bottom, and finally, she got in. I giggle to this day about that.

I went to a concert with my sister one time and ended up meeting a guy named Chad. He was twenty-two, and I was sixteen. He was so hot. He wasn't a boy like Justin; he was a man. Chad called the next day, and I invited him over to meet my dad.

"Mr. Thomas, I would love to take your daughter out." Chad reached out his hand.

"How old are you again?" my dad asked.

"Twenty-two, sir," he replied.

My dad then asked, "What's a twenty-two-year-old want with a sixteen-year-old?" Crossing his arms, his face was as cold as ice. I thought my dad was going to embarrass me again. Standing tall like a grizzly bear ready to attack my dad glared at Chad with curiosity.

Chad smiled. "Just time with your daughter. I really enjoy being with her."

"I bet you do." My dad walked over to his gun case. "Would you like something to drink, Chad?

"No, thank you." *I think Chad is too nervous to drink or eat anything. I thought.*

Dad opened his gun case and took out one of his huge shotguns. "You ever cleaned a shotgun?" He turned to Chad.

Chad turned into a human popsicle; he froze right where he stood. "Sir?" All the blood had rushed out of his face.

"Have a seat." Dad pointed to the couch right by his recliner. "I have three beautiful girls." My dad started to rub ointment on his gun.

"Yes, you do, sir." Chad started to shift in his seat.

"The good Lord knows I would hate to see the guy who hurt one of them."

"OMG!" I stormed off to find mom. "Momma, make him stop," I begged.

"You know your daddy's not gonna listen to me," she snickered. I went back into the living room where Chad sat on the hot seat. I was shocked to see him interested in how my dad cleaned his gun. Dad walked over to his gun case to place his gun back inside. He clicked the lock and turned to Chad.

"As long as you stay here at the house, you can date my daughter." I rolled my eyes.

"Really, Daddy."

My Dad looked at me, forehead wrinkled and eyebrows narrowed. "Or you cannot date at all."

"Daddy, please!" I threw myself on the couch by Chad.

"Oh, okay." He smiled. "Melissa!" The sound of my dad yelling for my sister meant one thing. Melissa came in, peeling an orange.

"Yes, Daddy."

"Your little sister wants to go out of the house with this fella." Chad quickly looked at me. I gave him a *just go with it* look. My sister was going to have to chaperone us.

Dad and Melissa were in a deep conversation. Melissa shrugged her shoulders. "Okay, I guess."

Chad and I had dated (with my sister watching) for 6 months. One night we were on the couch after everyone had gone to bed. He was sitting, and I was lying with my head in his lap. As I looked up at him, he had this weird look on his face.

"What?" I looked in his eyes.

"I want you to be my wife." He rubbed my ring finger. I jumped off that couch like a scolded hound.

"WHAT?" I asked.

"Shhhh." He covered my mouth with his hand. "You are going to wake up the whole house."

I sat down, and the living room walls began to close in on me. My eyes blinked fast. I was shocked. "What? I am sixteen!"

He gazed into my eyes. "I will love you forever."

I said, "No, I will not be the queen of your double-wide trailer!"

That song was popular at that time, so it was the first thing that popped in my mind and out of my mouth. I am thankful I dodged that bullet because I later found out he was very abusive. So, once again, my daddy protected me.

*****

When I turned seventeen, it was pure war at my house. I started to hang out with the wrong crowd and found myself smoking cigarettes, or at least trying to. I thought I was cool, even though I had no idea how to inhale.

My friend Stephanie sat on the back of a truck's tailgate on a sunny day, sipping Boone's wine. "You sure you don't want to try it?" She wrinkled up her nose.

"No, thank you," I shook my head.

"Are you going to school Monday?" She took another swig of the wine. My stomach rolled around with sickness.

"School," I sighed. "Yes. I have to go."

Every school day was the same thing over and over. I lay in bed. "Jody, get up." My mom pulled the covers off me.

"No," I snapped and pulled them back over my head.

"Fine, I will tell your dad when he gets home."

"Fine! Leave me alone and let me sleep."

"You are going to sleep your life away." And my mom slammed the door.

I murmured under the covers, "I would rather sleep my life away than be in school."

"If you live under my roof, you will follow my rules," my dad stood, chest poked out and pointing his finger at me. "Jody, you must go to school! You are grounded! No friends, no phone, and no TV. You will be there tomorrow; it isn't up for discussion."

"I can't wait to turn eighteen," I screamed. I was so angry at the whole world around me. Thinking back, I have to ask myself *why Jody? Why did you rush to get out of the home you were so sheltered in? You were so safe in! You were surrounded by people who loved you and protected you.*

*****

My dad was strict, and very set in his ways. When I was little there was no "time out"; you got your butt spanked, and I am a better person because of it. I respect people and I thank my dad for those hard lessons I had to learn.

When you are younger you don't really understand why certain things are the way they are. Growing up, our backyard was very embarrassing to me. My dad had old washers, dryers, refrigerators, cars; it looked like one big junk yard. We were at church one morning when this little old lady with grey hair and lines all over her face came up to my dad. "Thank you, Mr. Thomas, for fixing my washer. What do I owe you?" Her wrinkled hands reached into her purse.

"Oh no." My dad put his hand on hers. "You don't owe me anything." He smiled gently. It was then I sat in that church parking lot, the proudest daughter, and realized that one person's junk is another person's treasure.

Many a trip we rode in silence in my dad's pickup truck, but one time he said, "You know, Jody, I didn't grow up like you did." I looked out the window, rolling my eyes. Here we go again. "I work super hard to support this family." His face showed no emotion. "When I was younger my dad would take a 2X4 and beat me till I bled. It was hard, Jody." I later found out that he was abused as a child. "I am hard on you kids because I love you."

I continued to stare out the window at the trees flying by. "I thank God that He saved me, and I am not the mean man my dad was." Looking back, I can see how he tried to talk to me and tell me his life stories, but at that time, I just wouldn't listen. My stomach still turns in disgust at the teenager I was. What I wouldn't give to sit, watch and listen to my dad talk.

When my sister was little, she got into the cabinets and drank Red Devil Lye. I wasn't born yet, and I think she was one. The doctors put her in an oxygen tent at the hospital. My parents didn't know if she was going to live.

My mom had told Dad about Jesus before, but he wanted no part of Him. As my sister was in the oxygen tent, my daddy prayed to Jesus to please save her. He said, "I will put down the bottle and follow you the rest of my life."

My sister lived, and so did my daddy – he was born again. He did exactly what he said, stopped drinking and started following Jesus. He let go of the anger that had dwelled in him for years. He loved God, and everyone who knew him knew he did. He was kind and would do anything for anyone.

I fought all the time with my parents and one of my dad's favorite sayings was, "When you turn eighteen, you can do what you want." I think back to the horrible teen I was. With tears falling down my face, I am so upset at that selfish teenager I used to be.

I sat there in front of a decorated German chocolate cake with "18" on it and waited for my family to sing *Happy Birthday* to me. All my family members gathered around the table. I sat there, arms crossed, waiting for them to sing to me. I scanned the room. Mom was pouring sweet tea. Dad stood firm with no emotion. My sister Melissa moved her eyes from me to my dad. Melinda was leaning against the wall with big hair and a perfectly painted face. My Grandma June sat on the couch with my Grandpa sipping coffee. They sang "Happy birthday to you, happy birthday to you…."

I stood up, pushing my chair back from the table. I looked at my dad, finally, my face cold as ice. Then, with my birthday cake on the table, I yelled, "I'm eighteen and out of here!"

My dad's eyes narrowed as he stared at me. My mom begins to cry. "Jody, please." My grandma tried to grab my hand.

"Sorry, Grandma." I lowered my eyes. "I have waited a long time for this day."

My dad's face turned red. He rubbed his hands through his hair in frustration and yelled, "If you leave, don't come back."

I jutted my chin out in defiance. "Fine," I responded. "I don't want to come back anyway." I grabbed my stuff and walked out the door.

My mom looked at my dad with big tears in her eyes. "She has no idea what she is walking into."

My dad, with tears in his eyes and breathing heavily, looked at my mom. "She is about to find out the hard way." Little did they know that statement would prove to be so true. I would never walk back in that door the same way ever again.

I left home, a safe place, because I didn't want to follow the rules, rules that would protect me from the harsh, ugly world I never knew but was about to learn quickly. So many teenagers take off into the unknown because of the same reason.

I was a rebellious teenager, and I was going to do it my way. My way was the WRONG way! When you are young, you think you know it all, but I am here to tell you that isn't true. You will see as you read this book just how dangerous the real world can be.

Chapter Four

RUNNING INTO DANGER

After leaving home, I moved in with my aunt and uncle who lived about forty-five minutes away. They didn't have strict rules, but I found out quickly why my dad did. I fought with my aunt too. *My mom is way cooler,* I thought. *I'm not happy here either.*

I got a job as a receptionist at a carpet place that lasted maybe one week. They were nice there, but boring. I did buy myself a red car (with help from my uncle) and thought that was the best thing ever. I was going everywhere in that car, running the roads. One cold morning I was headed home when smoke begin to pour from under the hood. The check engine light was flashing at me. *I bet I can make it,* I thought. I mean, I didn't know how to check an engine, so I continued down the road.

BOOM! My car stopped and flames began shooting up. OMG! I jumped out of the car. A nice gentleman stopped behind me. His face wrinkled with concern, he turned and faced me. "You blew your motor, ma'am," he said in a southern accent. *CRAP!* I thought. I called my uncle, and he had it towed to the house. Lesson learned: the check engine light means…check the engine. Thank God my uncle had a buddy who was a mechanic.

It wasn't horrible there with my aunt and uncle. I could come and go as I pleased, and I loved that at first. I did have to get a job to pay back my uncle and fast. I searched the classifieds and found the perfect job.

After filling out an application, I sat across from a huge man with thick glasses who was smoking a cigar under his mustache, moving from side to side in his big office chair. "Why should we hire you?" He leaned his elbows on his desk.

I sat tall, shoulders back and with confidence replied, "Because I am a fast learner and a people person."

"Hmm." he picked up my resume. "Well, you're not qualified, but you do have a good personality and that is important for the receptionist to have." He leaned back, twirling his mustache. "You got the job. We are going to have to train you."

I jumped up and grabbed his giant hand. "Thank you. Thank you so much!"

"We like dresses and skirts here." He grinned behind his big mustache.

"Not a problem," I replied as I floated out the door.

Mr. Mustache's business was booming, and my paycheck was fat. Ring! Ring! I would answer and connect the call. People came in and out dressed in business suits and some men wore bow ties. The massive desk I sat behind was in the shape of a half circle. The only items I needed were the big switchboard that blinked at me constantly and my pen and paper to take notes. I was the first person you saw when you walked through those big glass doors.

"I am the important one," I smiled to myself. I worked every other Saturday which I never minded because the phone hardly rang at all. One day as I was sitting in my big chair doodling on the note pad, the glass doors opened. In walked this tall, gorgeous guy with black flowing hair, strong jaw, and muscles showing through this tee shirt. I almost fell over as he slowly approached my desk.

"Good morning." He grinned, showing the most beautiful teeth.

"Good morning, Sir." I smiled back. "How may I help you?"

"I don't know." He leaned in, put his elbows on my desk, and rested his handsome face in his hands. "You are so beautiful I forgot why I am here." I blushed ten shades of red. He stood back up. "Is Mr. Smith in?" I gazed into his eyes, lost in a daydream of us on the beach, hand in hand. "Ma'am!"

I jolted back to reality. "I am so sorry. Who was it you wanted to see?" A huge grin came across his face. "Mr. Smith? Oh yes." Still blushing, I said, "let me get him for you." *Of all days for Mr. Smith to be in his office, I thought. Handsome and I could have talked for hours.* After he went back to see Mr. Smith, I kept rolling my chair backwards to peek down the hall to see if he was coming back.

I was leaning down under my desk to get my lipstick when I heard the visitor's sexy voice. "What are you doing down there?" I jerked my head up and BAM hit the bottom of the desk. Ouch! "You okay?" He leaned over the desk to get a better look. I wanted to climb all the way under it I was so embarrassed. I was brushing the hair out of my face when I saw him grab a post-it note and pen off my desk. He flashed his pearly whites at me. "May I have your number?"

OMG. I blushed again. *This hot guy wants MY number. Thank God I live with my aunt and uncle. Surely my dad would embarrass me.* "Sure." I took the pen and begin to write. He took the note and tucked it into his front pocket.

"Thank you." He patted the pocket with a smile.

"No, thank you." I smiled back.

*****

I waited patiently for my Ken doll to call. "OMG, he is so HOT!" I told my girlfriend on the phone.

"How old is he?" she asked, while smacking on her gum.

"Early twenties I guess. I don't know, and I don't care." I giggled back to her. Just then it happened – the phone beeped. "OMG the phone is beeping!"

"Click over, duh."

"OKAY." With my heart racing I did. "Hello?"

"Hello, beautiful." The words were like smooth silk.

"Hi," I replied. "Can you hold on one second please?" I spoke calmly.

"Sure, I can, beautiful."

"Hello? Hey girl who is it?"

"EEEEK," I squealed, "it's him!"

"Ouch, that was my ear, Jody!"

"Well, that is payback for all the smacking gum you do in mine!"

"Talk later," she giggled.

"Talk later," I replied. This was the first phone call of many I had with Trek. He was so kind and sweet to me. I told him everything about me from my favorite food to how I just moved out because my parents were so unfair.

He also told me everything about him. He came from a very wealthy family and was born into money. "It didn't change who I am though." His words made my heart flutter. "I have waited my whole life to find my princess and now I have."

"Whatever," I giggled into the phone. "You have only known me a couple of months and that is only on the phone."

"I know," he said. "I see how beautiful your heart is. You are the complete package. I can't wait to show you off to my parents; they will love you. We could go ride horses on my ranch."

"As you know, I love horses." I couldn't hide the excitement.

"I know, baby," he whispered softly. "So, do you think you could enjoy your life with me?"

"Are you kidding? Yes!" My heart raced fast.

"Jody, I have to tell you something."

"What?" I paced back and forth across my bedroom.

"I love you and want to be with you forever." I almost dropped the phone.

"You do?"

"Yes, Jody. Do you love me?" he asked softly.

"I love you too." Excitement filled my whole body. "I can't wait to see you again, to hold you close." I couldn't hold back my feelings anymore.

"I count the days, princess."

"When?"

"Patience, my love. Like I told you, I am a busy man, but I promise as soon as I can I will come get you."

I threw myself on my bed, holding my pillow close. "Okay," I whispered.

A week later I received the most gorgeous roses delivered to me at work. The card read, "I have a surprise for you. Love, Trek." I floated through the large building into the kitchen to get some water.

"Wow! Those are some flowers," Mr. Mustache grinned.

"Thank you!" I began to run water in the crystal vase. I could hardly wait to get home and wait for Trek's call. Around 6 p.m. the phone rang, "Hello?" I answered, super excited to talk to my man.

"Hello, gorgeous." I slumped down in a chair. "I got your surprise today."

He chuckled into the phone. "That's not the surprise."

I sat up straight. "What?"

"The surprise is I am flying in tonight for a cocktail party, and YOU are my date."

I jumped up out of the chair and did a happy dance around the room. "Really?"

"Yes, beautiful, I want you to meet all my friends. I have even better news, princess." Excitement filled his voice.

"OMG! What?" I pleaded.

"I told my parents about you and they are super excited to meet you soon."

"I love you, I love you, I love you," I said, still dancing around the room.

"Get dressed and look hot for me, princess."

"Oh, I will. Bye for now." I hung up the phone and began going through all my little black dresses to pick out the perfect one. As I was sitting in front of my vanity putting on makeup, the phone rang. "I will get it," I yelled down the hall. "Hello?"

"Beautiful, something came up. I only have a minute."

"Okay," I replied, frowning.

"Nothing bad, silly. I just can't meet you at the parking lot. My friend will meet you there instead. It is after hours, so I am sure his will be the only car there."

"Umm, okay." The pit of my stomach fell.

"He is so nice! You will love him, silly girl. He is going to pick you up to take you to the party."

"So excited to finally see you, handsome."

"I am more excited, princess. Meet him there at 7. I love you. See you soon."

I put on my sexy black dress and pink high heels and went rushing out the door

As I approached the parking lot, a few street lights were all I saw where the one car was parked. My heart beat fast. One step at a time I slowly walked up to the car. I opened the door and there sat a big guy who took up the whole seat. "Hey. You must be Jody. You are very beautiful, just like I was told. Trek gave me the honors of picking you up since he is running late."

Then I had it – that gut feeling that told me not to get in the car with him. I shook my head to shake off the thought. I wanted to see Trek so badly, and this was the only way. If I acted like I was better than his friend, Trek may never speak to me again. "It is nice to meet you too," I grinned back and got into the car.

We drove for what seemed like miles when we turned into an old beat up motel that had about 30 to 40 rooms, one floor only. The paint was chipped off in most places and rust had taken over the building. The weeds were winning as they popped up everywhere in the cement. I tried to take in every detail around me, but I was getting sicker by the minute. I murmured, "Where are we?"

That is when he took out a gun and placed it on his lap. "No more questions," he grunted.

What is going on? My mind raced with questions and my heart raced with anxiety. I tried to pull at my dress to make it longer to cover my knees. Here I am all dressed up to walk into a party and instead we are parked outside one of the worst motels I have ever seen. I was tricked. I started to rub my palms together as the tears welled up in my eyes.

"Please let me go," I begged.

"Shut up," he snapped, never taking his eyes off the motel we sat in front of. He made sure no one was around. After about ten minutes of sitting there, he turned and leaned over to me. "We're going to walk in together, and if you run or scream, you die."

By this time, I was crying so hard, I couldn't breathe.

"Quit crying," he said, his voice menacing.

"I can't," I sobbed.

He walked over and opened the door. "Get out!" I could see the gun in his jacket pocket pointed right at me. I slowly slid out of the car. He turned me around in front of him and I felt the cold metal on my back.

He nudged me to a door to one of the rooms. He opened the door and it felt like a horror movie and I was the leading star. The room was dirty, and the smell of cigarette smoke was strong. All I could think of was *if I scream no one will save me*. I felt the vomit come up in my throat and I just swallowed it back down. I was frozen in fear, scared to move, paralyzed, sitting on this stain-filled comforter.

He sat down next to me, placing his hand on my bare knee. My whole body shook. He began to kiss my neck, and I gasped at him, "Please don't, I'm a virgin."

He moved the gun closer, so it touched my back and continued to kiss my neck. I felt so helpless. There was nothing I could do, and no one to save me. What I had saved for the man I was going to marry was about to be taken by a stranger in a dirty motel room. *Where is God? Why doesn't He save me? Why is this happening to me?*

He placed his lips on mine, and it took everything inside me not to throw up. I was a teenager who knew nothing about what was about to happen to me.

"Get undressed," he ordered.

I begged again, "Please. Please don't do this to me. Please don't hurt me! Please!"

His voice was gruff. "Stop talking and do what I tell you."

When I refused to get undressed, I felt him undo the zipper down my back. "Stop!" I tried to fight him off with what little strength I had. This angered him.

"I can kill you and not blink an eye." Picking up his gun he ordered me again to get undressed. I knew I had no choice as I slipped my dress down off my body. I stood in front of him naked and terrified. "Lie down." He began to undress. This huge wolf was about to attack an innocent scared sheep.

As he crawled over me, I whispered, "Please let me stay a virgin. I have been a virgin for eighteen years. Please don't take that from me."

"No more talking." His voice was now husky. It didn't matter what I said; his mind was not changing. This is the evil world that existed for me in that moment. This is what my dad had been trying so hard to protect me from. No one could save me, and I had to accept what was happening to me against my will.

Once he got on top of me, it felt like a huge dark shadow was suffocating me. His weight was almost unbearable. He propped himself over me and took my hand and made me feel him. It was the first time I had ever touched any man there. "Touch it. Make it hard," he said.

"I don't know how," I cried.

He then proceeded to do it himself with my hand under his.

"Please stop," I cried.

The next thing that happened is a pain I can't put into words. It hurt so bad, and I prayed to God to please let it stop.

He was sweating on me, and each drop felt like boiling water hitting my body, burning every piece of me. He went deeper, and fear went in with him. He went deeper still, and hate went in with him. He went even deeper, and anger went in with him. As he went deeper, innocence went away. I was no longer the same. He raped me, he took everything I had saved for all those years. He took what I had saved for my husband one day. I thought about when someone gives you a beautiful porcelain doll. You cherish it and keep it safe until someone comes along and breaks it into little pieces. No matter how much glue you use the doll is broken.

As he went into the bathroom, I lay there lifeless. Every part of me shrieked in pain. I wondered if Trek would rescue me, but he never did. The huge black shadow came out of the bathroom wiping his hands with a towel.

"Get some sleep. Don't even think of leaving or I will kill you and your whole family. Thanks to Trek I know EVERYTHING about you, princess." He lay down beside me, placing his huge sweaty arm around me with the gun in his hand lying by my head.

I prayed to God so desperately to please tell me what to do. I was so scared he was going to kill me. I stared at that mold-filled ceiling and saw cockroaches crawl across the wall that made my whole body shiver.

That was the longest night of my life. I lay next to a monster and listened to the worst noise ever: his snoring. I thought about taking a pillow and sitting on his face until his chest stopped moving up and down, but the gun at my head reminded me that wasn't an option.

I prayed so hard all night long. Growing up and all those Sunday School classes were about to pay off. Psalm 23 4. I begin to whisper, "Yea, though I walk through the valley of death, I will fear no evil; for thou art with me; thy rod and thy staff they comfort me." *God is with me,* I whispered to myself. *God can make a way where there is no way.* I begin to feel hope. *God please show me the way.* It was then my sister Melissa came to my mind. Yes! I thought. *Perfect!* I didn't think he would ever wake up, but as the sun peeked through the dirty window I felt his arm move. He woke up, and anxiety rushed through my body. I was so exhausted and sore.

He walked into the bathroom and I got up, grabbed my dress and put it on. I sat on the edge of the bed legs shaking and still praying. He came out of the bathroom, naked and nasty, and glared at me.

I begged, "Please, not again." He paused and went back into the bathroom. The motel phone rang, and I jumped.

"Yeah," he snapped. "Yes! Yes!" And he slammed the phone down. He began to grab his clothes and I breathed a sigh of relief. Thank God, he didn't rape me again. As he was getting dressed, in my most confident voice I said.

"Good morning, I need to go home now."

He turned to me, suddenly walked over, picked up his gun tapped me on the shoulder, "What did you say?"

I repeated the verse that I had said all night in my mind. *I will fear no evil. God is with me.* It took everything I had to repeat it. "I need to go home now."

His brow narrowed as a frown appeared on his face. "No!"

I smiled and forced myself to be kind to him. "I promise to meet you again."

He turned, and his glare shot right through me. I thought I was about to die.

His eyebrows furrowed in confusion. "Why would I let you go?"

"Because I will come back," I assured him.

"You will?" he asked, throwing his head back laughing.

"Yes, I promise," I stood firm. "My sister works for the Highway Patrol, and if I don't get to my car, she'll report it stolen." I had told her about meeting Trek.

He started to rub his hand back and forth across his big head. "Does Trek know where your sister works?" He grabbed my arms tight and his anger-filled eyes pierced into mine.

"No, I didn't tell him." Tears begin to roll down my face. He started to pace the room back and forth with this gun in hand. I could tell with every step he took he was getting more frustrated.

"I need to think," he kept repeating. "Think. Think. Think." Stress covered his face and I sat there, eyes closed, praying that he wouldn't shoot me.

"Fine," he said, I jumped. "But you better come back as promised." *Thank you, Jesus,* I whispered to myself.

"What?" he snapped.

"Thank you." I somewhat smiled.

"I am not taking you back to your car, I will call you a cab. Speak of this to no one or I will kill you."

"I know." I shook my head up and down.

He handed me two twenty-dollar bills. "This will be enough to get you to your car."

"I can pay for it," I said.

"Whatever." He shoved the money back into his pocket. I already felt dirty enough and the last thing I wanted was his dirty money. When I heard the horn honk it sounded like freedom. I jumped up to open the door and he grabbed my arm hard. "See you soon he smirked."

"See you soon," I replied.

When we pulled up to my car, I could feel freedom getting closer. I saw men differently now and was thankful the cab driver didn't try to hurt me. "Thank you," I replied as I handed him the money.

"Have a good day, ma'am," he smiled.

Once I got in my car, I felt nothing but relief. I was still alive. I sat there behind the wheel thinking of how much my life had changed in just 24 hours. Tears begin to flood my eyes and I couldn't breathe. I shook my hands and took a deep breath. My mind searched where to go. I remember praying so hard for God to please protect me. I was so scared of being followed. I decided on a hospital that was thirty minutes away.

I watched behind me the entire time I drove, which felt like hours. Every time a car got behind me my heart would race faster. Anxiety filled my whole body. *OMG! I didn't die* played over and over in my mind.

I drove straight to the hospital; my body in so much pain. As I entered through its glass doors, I walked toward the front desk to ask where to go if I just got raped. Then I heard his voice so loudly in my mind, saying, "I will kill your family."

I turned and went straight to the nursery. So much happiness was all around newborn babies. I pulled my legs up to my chest. "Are you all right?" a nurse asked.

"Yes," I nodded my head. "Just tired."

What if I get pregnant, I thought? *What if I have this man's baby inside me?* I hurt so bad between my legs that it was painful to even sit. I shifted from side to side. The pain was excruciating.

"Are you okay, sweetie?" a lady asked me. "You look like you got ants in your pants." Little did she know; down there was so sore like a million ants had actually attacked me.

"I'm fine," I said, but I knew she could tell I was lying. I'm sure my face was pale, and I wondered if I had blood anywhere on my clothes. I hadn't looked in a mirror and had no idea what I looked like.

I sat in that hospital all day trying to figure out my next move. I didn't want to go back to my aunt's house because I had given all the details about where I lived to Trek. *Trek, that jerk! Who was he? Where had this new guy come from?* Confusion made my head spin like a top.

Then fear shifted through my bones. I told Trek everything about me. This guy said he would kill me and my family. *Where can I go? Where is safe right now?* I remembered my friend Jennifer had said I could stay at her place anytime.

I gave her a call. "Hello," she answered.

"Jennifer, it's me. My aunt and I just had this huge fight. Can I please stay with you?"

"Of course," she replied. "We are just sitting down to eat."

Dinner popped into my mind. Tears begin to fall. I remembered when life was so simple, such as sitting down to dinner together when Dad got home from work. "Okay, I'm on my way." I let out a sigh of relief as I hung up the phone.

When I got to her house, her mom greeted me like always. "Hey, sweetheart, you hungry?"

"No thanks," I said.

"Wow! You look rough," Jennifer spouted with a laugh. "It must have been some party last night."

"You have no idea," I murmured. I gave her a quick smile and told her I really wanted to take a shower.

"Sure," she said. I walked as fast as I could down the hallway, the tears coming faster and faster. When I reached the bathroom, I couldn't get the clothes off fast enough. I felt so dirty. I needed to get that man off me.

I got the water so hot, you could have boiled something in it. I stood in that shower and cried so hard as water poured onto my body. I looked down and saw blood run down my legs into the drain.

I finally could no longer stand. My legs collapsed, and I fell to the shower floor. Images of him on top of me flashed like a picture show through my mind. The deeper inside me he went, the harder I scrubbed. My skin was so red, I had scrubbed the skin right off. He took more than just my virginity. He took my innocence. He took my feelings and numbed me of my emotions. He also inserted in me fear, anger, guilt, and the list goes on.

"I can't get him off," I cried harder and harder. I scrubbed my skin until I was too tired to move my arm. *I feel so dirty no matter how clean the soap makes me,* I thought. I sat on the shower floor and cried so hard that I threw up.

A knock on the door made my heart and body jump! "Are you okay in there?" Jennifer asked.

"Yes, sorry. I just felt a little too dirty," I yelled back.

"Okay, well, dinner is ready if you want to eat with us." The thought of food made we want to vomit again.

"I'm not hungry!" I yelled back. Then, "Hey Jenn. Do you have any long-sleeve pajamas I can sleep in?" I knew my arms were beginning to bruise from him grabbing me.

"Sure," she yelled back. "In the top drawer."

I put on her cute Hello Kitty pajamas and cried again. I knew I would no longer be a Hello Kitty girl. Instead, I was a stray, ugly cat that no one wanted. I sat on her big canopy bed surrounded by stuffed animals. I couldn't tell what kind of wallpaper she had since her room was full of cute boy posters. The white carpet and white dresser looked so pure. Everything was neat and in its place. Several ribbons and trophies sat perfectly on a shelf.

I bet her parents are so proud of her, I thought as I lay back on the bed. Chills ran through my body and I sat up right away. *Will I never be able to lean back on a bed like normal people?* The whole room wasn't that big, but all I could do was stare at the window waiting for someone to come through it. I lay there like a fly waiting for a spider to attack.

Is he coming after me? Is someone else going to hurt me or get me? I rocked back and forth nervously as the thoughts ran through my mind. I walked over to Jenn's vanity and picked up her brush. As I looked in the mirror brushing my hair, the tears begin to fall. All I could think was that I couldn't believe what just happened to me.

Jenn came strolling in with a huge smile on her face. "Guess what?" she asked, throwing herself across the bed and grabbing her favorite sparkly pillow.

"What?" I turned from the mirror.

"Felix asked me out! I am so excited!"

"Felix from church?" I asked

"Yes." She grabbed the hairbrush and started to sing into it.

"Annnnd then he kissed me. Kissed me in a way that I have never been kissed before." It was lines from our favorite late-night popcorn movie.

"That's awesome." I patted her on the back.

Two days ago, I would have jumped up and sang and danced around the room with her. That was no longer me. Instead I was sore, sad, and miserable inside.

"OMG, you're jealous." She rolled her eyes.

"I am not," I snapped back.

"Well then, why are you not happy for me?" She frowned.

"Long night," I whispered.

"You and Trek get into a fight." She flipped her hair. To hear his name made my blood boil inside.

"YES! Never speak his name again," I blurted out, tears flowing down my face. She walked over and wrapped her skinny arms around me.

"I am sorry. I know how much you loved him."

"I need to get some sleep." I crawled into her big bed.

. She shrugged. "Okay. I'm going to go sleep in the guestroom."

"No!" I cried.

"OMG," she jumped back. "What is it?"

"Please, will you sleep beside me?" I almost pleaded. She jumped back in shock. "Like when we were little and had slumber parties."

She giggled and jumped into the bed. "Silly girl! Night."

"Good night," I replied. But it wasn't a good night at all. My thoughts were many, and I didn't sleep much. I woke several times throughout the night. I would sit straight up in the bed, my heart beating out of my chest. I would see Jenn's cross nightlight and turn to see this beautiful blonde sound asleep. I hated the feeling of waking up and not knowing where I was.

"Where am I?" This was one of many, many night terrors I would have starting at that point in my life.

I was out of bed before the sun came up. Thank God, Jenn and I were the same size because I borrowed her clothes to leave in. I pulled my hair back into a pony tail, slipped on Jenn's flip flops and walked out the door. I got in my car with the black trash bag I had stuck my dirty clothes in, even my cute pink heels. I knew I would never look at them the same. As the car started, I quickly looked all around me but there was nothing but darkness. Jenn lived in the woods. I locked the doors and said a prayer. I took a deep breath and pulled out of her long driveway.

My aunt lived a good hour away and that needed to be my first stop. As I pulled up to the house all the cars were gone. *I am so thankful they are all gone to work*. I parked my car and popped the trunk. I walked into the house, my heart racing, throwing clothes into trash bags as fast as I could. The phone rang, and I jumped. The answering machine clicked on and one of my aunt's friends left her a message. Thank God it wasn't Trek.

Why? Why did he lie to me? What kind of game were they playing? A sick one. I shook my head. No time for that I must get out of here.

As I was walking out the door the phone rang again. I waited for the machine to pick it up and heard Stan's voice. Stan was mid-thirties. He was friends with one of the guys at the office and that is how we met. He was always so nice to me and I had gone to lunch with him a few times. We were friends and he called me sometimes just to chitchat about life. I felt horrible leaving and not letting anyone know. I picked up the phone. "Hi, Stan."

"Hey Jody! There you are." I looked at the clock. Crap, it was almost nine. "Sorry, I must have slept in; I am not feeling the best." I coughed into the phone.

"Oh, wow. I wanted you to come by the office if you had time."

"What for?" Curiosity got the better of me.

"A gift," he replied. "It's at my office. Will you please swing by and get it?"

"A gift?" I asked.

He chuckled through the phone. "Yes, nothing big, just something that made me think of you."

"Okay," I paused. "I guess."

"Can you come over now?"

"Sure," I replied, and hung up the phone.

I got the rest of my garbage bags and left a note on the counter for my aunt and uncle. The note read: "Being on my own is not what I thought it would be. Thank you for letting me stay here but I need to move back home." I turned and picked up the phone.

"Mom. It's me."

"Hey Jody, how are you?"

"Not good." I sobbed. "I don't like it here; can I please come home?" The phone went silent. "Mom, please," I whispered.

"Jody, you know what your daddy said when you left."

"I know," I sniffled. I couldn't hold back. I begin to cry so hard I could barely breathe.

"Okay, Baby. If it is that bad come home. I will deal with your dad."

"Thank you, Mom. I have one stop and then I will be there. Give me about three hours."

"OK, sweetheart, see you soon." I hung up the phone and walked out the door, wiping the tears from my eyes.

Stan told me where his office was located and that I had to push a code for the door to open. When I got there, sure enough I touched the space like he said, and a door magically appeared.

He had a huge office. There was pure glass everywhere and an oversized couch sat in the middle. The view of the water through the windows was amazing. His large desk covered in papers looked like a huge mess. He walked over and picked up crystal candle holders. "These are for you." He handed me the gorgeous candle holders.

"You are so sweet, Stan. Thank you so much," I reached out to hug him like I had a million times, but this time the vibe was different. He grabbed my arms.

"All I get is a hug for crystal?" he whispered in my ear. He touched my hair and my whole body tensed up.

"What are you doing?" I asked.

"You know you have been flirting with me." He pulled me closer into him. He started being forceful and kissing my neck.

"Leave me alone!" I screamed. He placed his finger on my mouth to hush me.

"Just relax," he said, his breath on my skin.

Anger began to grow deep inside me. I got as close to his ear as I could. "Go ahead, rape me, Stan. You will be number two. I was raped last night too!"

His face went pale. "What?"

"Yes, so if you want to go inside me, know that someone dirtier and nastier than you were inside me last night. You might get a gift yourself, Stan." I threw the crystal candle sticks against the wall and they shattered into pieces all over the marble floor.

"Get out!" he screamed. I pushed a button, and once again a door appeared. My heart raced as I ran to my car, climbed in, and looked around to make sure I was all alone. The tears began to fall. *Did that really almost happen again?* My face went pale, and I threw up out the side window of the car. *I can't believe this is my life.*

I drove for miles trying to listen to the radio, but every song made me cry. I pulled up to the house that was once my safe place. I punched my steering wheel in anger. Stupid girl. I knocked on the door, and my mom opened it with a huge smile.

"Hello, baby." I hugged her so tight. I cried so hard. I was trembling in her arms.

"What is wrong, Jody?" She held me tighter.

"I just missed you, Mom." I buried my head into her shoulder.

"I missed you too, baby." Tears filled her eyes. "Are you hungry, sweetie?"

"No, thank you. I can't eat. Will you make me a pallet on the couch like you used to when I was sick?"

"Are you sick?" My mom's face looked puzzled.

"No, Mom, just tired." And I removed my shoes.

I knew when my dad drove up he would see my car. He walked in while I was still lying on the couch. "What are you doing here?" His voice was low and stern.

I sat up slowly. "Daddy, I am sorry, can I please come home?"

His face didn't budge as he walked into the kitchen. Mom always had dinner on the table when Daddy got home. My oldest sister was married and out of the house and my middle sister was less than pleased that I was back. "Jody," my dad yelled. "Get in here and eat your dinner."

"I'm not hungry." I replied.

"I didn't ask you if you were hungry."

I walked into our bright yellow kitchen and Mom had made mac 'n cheese, drumsticks, and green beans. I filled my plate and sat down with my family. We all joined hands and said grace. We ate in silence, and it wasn't long until dad addressed the elephant in the room…me. He dropped his fork onto his empty plate. I jumped. He crossed his arms and leaned back in his chair.

"I told you that if you leave, don't come back."

I swallowed the lump in my throat. "Yes, Sir."

"I remember you saying, 'Fine, I didn't want to ever come back.'" I sat frozen to my chair. "So why are you here?"

I couldn't hold the tears back. "I was wrong, and I need a place to stay," I sobbed.

Saying nothing, my dad pushed his chair back from the table and walked outside. "Let him cool off," my mom smiled, as she cleared the table. "You know your daddy isn't going to put you out on the streets."

An hour later my dad came back inside. He sat in his recliner and started to take his work boots off. "You can stay here, but you will get a job, and you will follow my rules."

"Thank you, Daddy." I reached down and wrapped my arms around his neck.

My sister Melissa and I shared a room for years, but since I left, she had her own room now. I stood in her door full of fear and worry; the thought of sleeping in a room alone petrified me. I lay in that bed for as long as I could stand it and then I crept down the hallway to my sister's room. When I opened the door, the hall light shone in her room. She opened her eyes. "What are you doing Jody?"

"Can I please sleep with you, Melissa?"

"No, Jody, go back to your own room."

"No," I snapped back. All I could think was *they know where my family lives. What if they break in and take me? What if they break in and kill my whole family?* Fear shot through my whole body. "No!" I whispered loudly. "I want to sleep with you."

"Then you can sleep on the floor." She covered her head with the blankets.

I took my sleeping bag and placed it on the floor at the foot of her bed. I did try to sneak into her bed, but she had a waterbed, so each time I tried to get in her bed, the water would float around.

"Go to sleep," she said, but sleep didn't exist for me anymore. There was no way I could sleep, so I laid curled up at the foot of her bed and cried. Every little noise made me jump. *What if it's him? What if he kills my whole family?* The thought made me toss and turn in my sleeping bag. Would I ever feel safe again? I would never be emotionally the same again.

If I could turn back time, I would have awakened my sister. I would have told her what had happened to me. She would have held me and protected me. That wasn't possible, though – I knew that.

When I awoke the next day, my dad insisted I had to go to work, so I did. I got a job at Plump Pals right away. Plump Pals was a small grocery store in the center of town. Bobby was the manager. He was a good-looking guy in his mid-thirties with an athletic build. "You got the job if you want it." Bobby smiled across his desk.

"Yes, I do." I jumped up to shake his hand.

I didn't mind being a cashier; it was fun. I loved how sweet the other employees were to me. I worked right by the front door, and every time those double doors opened, I held my breath, praying I wouldn't see the two men I feared the most.

I got a second job as a nanny for Bobby. "My wife is so stressed out," he told me one night at closing. "I just wish I could get her some help."

I shifted from one foot to the other. "You mean a nanny?"

"Yes." He turned and looked at me. "I can't pay a lot, but it would be some extra money."

My mind instantly went to *could this be a safe place for me?* I thought the manager was so cool and he really loved his family. "I will do it." I smiled at him.

"What do you know about being a nanny?" He crossed his arms.

"I love kids," I laughed.

"Let me talk to my wife and get back to you." The next day Bobby came in all smiles. "My wife wants to meet you."

That evening I went over to their house and Bobby's wife loved me. "You got the job!" She high-fived me.

I stayed over at Bobby and Gail's a lot. They had four of the cutest kids I had ever seen: a set of two-year-old twins, a beautiful blonde four-year-old boy, and a sassy five-year-old girl. I must admit they were good-looking parents. Gail had a body that would stop traffic; she used to model back in the day. She was 5' feet 7" and built like an hour glass. She was a stay-at-home mom with four children – a full-time job for anyone.

I liked going over there. The kids were so precious to watch. They kept me busy playing hide and seek or chasing them all over the place. I stayed at my house sometimes and at Bobby and Gail's other times. The kids brought me joy and, let's be honest, I wasn't feeling much joy at all. I did feel safe there, as safe as one can feel.

One night after we all clocked out at work, one of my friends, Mandy, said, "Grab a buggy. Let's go shopping."

"That's stealing," I said.

"No, it's not. Just ask Bobby. They order extra, so it's all good."

"Get what you want," Bobby said, and winked at me.

I have the coolest boss ever! "Okay," I said and grabbed a buggy to start shopping. And boy, did we shop! I got everything from shampoo to cereal.

When I got home, my sister was awake. "What is all that?" she asked, staring at my bags.

"Nothing," I said, unloading all my goodies on the bed.

"Jody, did you pay for that?"

"Not exactly." I shrugged my shoulders. "They have extra, so we got to take it home."

My sister put me in the car and drove me back to Plump Pals. I sat arms crossed and mad as a hornet. "This is so stupid," I grunted.

"You will thank me when you're not in jail." She shook her head.

It was after hours and Bobby was still in his office. I tapped on the big glass doors. Bobby opened the doors with a huge smile. "You miss me so much you ready to work again?"

"No!" My sister blurted. "She is here to return all this. We were raised not to steal." I was so embarrassed.

All the color drained from Bobby's face. "I thought you did pay for it." He put his hands on his hips.

My eyes widened in shock. "But…"

"No buts," he cut me off. He touched my back and escorted me through the store. "Just put everything back, Jody, and we will not have to call the police."

"WHAT?" You could have knocked me over with a feather. As my sister was placing things on another aisle, Bobby leaned over and whispered, "Our secret, remember?"

"Oh." I blushed. I was so mad at Melissa, but little did I know she saved me from jail. The whole place was being watched, and I had no idea.

*****

When I got home one day, my dad was watching M*A*S*H*. He loved that show. "Jody, one of your friends keeps calling and hanging up the phone," my dad grunted. "I am not playing these little games with them." My heart raced. I knew exactly who it was. As I walked into our yellow kitchen to get some water the phone rang.

"I'll get it," I said. "Hello." My voice shook.

"You lied to me," he whispered. I dropped the water and the cup bounced across the floor. Fear ripped through my body like a tidal wave. He had found me. "I told you I would kill you and your family. You think I am playing little girl. Don't you?" No, not at all!

"I've been working," I whispered. "It wasn't on purpose. My sister has been watching me like a hawk. I wanted to give it some time before I came back!"

"Time's Up, Jody!"

I slid down the wall, tears beginning to roll down my face. I couldn't breathe. I had to pull it together. What if someone walked in. How would I explain how upset I was? No longer a little girl, I must behave like a woman. I cleared my throat. "Okay. When and where?" I asked boldly.

I understand when people read this book, they will judge me. I understand. I have judged myself for twenty-plus years, but it was what I had to do to survive. I wanted to lie about this part, but God spoke to me and said to tell the true story. Someone needs to know it. I did what I had to do to survive. Unless you have walked in my shoes, you can't understand the fear of why I had to go back to the man who raped me.

"The same motel as before, 8 p.m. sharp!"

Trying hard for my voice not to shake, I replied, "I will be there."

Then I heard him click his gun. "You better be. Oh, and Jody?"

"Yes?"

"Look pretty for me."

My stomach dropped. "Okay," I gulped. The phone went dead. I stood and hung up the phone on the wall, then cleaned up the spilled water on the floor. *What have I done with my life? What am I going to do?* I thought of my spare key. I never used it and it was only in case I got locked out of my car. I went into my old bedroom, my hands still shaking, to get that key. God told me to get that key.

I am not sure why, but showers brought me comfort. Maybe because you cry and cry and no one hears you. Maybe because they soothe you. Maybe it is the sound. Melissa beat on the door. "Jody, come on. We need to shower too, ya know?" I was done and turned off the water, reaching for the towel to dry off. I wanted to make sure she couldn't tell I was crying.

As a family, we all sat around the living room and watched TV.

When the picture messed up someone had to go outside and turn the big huge antenna attached to the house. I used to hate this job, but I needed to be by myself without curious eyes on me. "I will go out and hold the antenna." I jumped off the couch.

My sister's forehead wrinkled in confusion. "Really, Jody?"

"Yes." I was out the door before anyone could stop me. As I stood outside turning this huge antenna, the tears falling down my face, I said a prayer. *God, I know I have really gotten myself into a mess. I also know that you can make a way where there is no way. This seems to be a no-way situation. Thank you, God, for making a way. Amen.*

That night Melissa let me sleep in her waterbed beside her. "Are you crying, Jody?"

"No, I just have allergies."

"Go to sleep, Sis, and don't move too much, okay?"

"Okay." I half smiled. Little did Melissa know I wouldn't sleep much at all, just lie there and pray.

The next day might have been sunny and bright for some, but it was super dark in the world for me. I watched the clock, and it seemed like the day crept by. Many times, I thought of telling Melissa what happened. She works for the Police, she could protect me, but I would shake off the thought; he would kill us if I did.

I walked into the living room where Mom was watching her TV shows. "I am going to nanny tonight for Bobby and Gail."

"Ok, sweetie. Will you be back tomorrow?"

"I am not sure, Mom." I picked up my duffle bag and slung it over my shoulder. I hugged my mom so tight. "I love you so much Momma."

"I love you too, baby. My goodness, you would think you were never going to see me again by that hug. Jody, are you sure you're okay?"

"Sorry, Mom, just emotional. It's that time of the month for me."

My mom smiled the sweetest smile and walked me out to my car. "See you soon, baby." She waved bye as I backed out of the driveway, waving and throwing kisses back at her.

My body shook as I pulled back into that motel. I knocked on the door. It opened, and there he stood. "You are a smart girl," he grinned and held the door open.

"I don't have much of a choice," I murmured. Walking into the motel this time I looked at things through different eyes. I noticed he was a big man. *I bet he isn't very athletic,* I thought. I noticed candy bar wrappers on the floor. *I bet he is very unhealthy. The harder he works out the more exhausted he will become.* It was then I started to make an escape plan in my mind.

No gun. I began to undress. His eyebrows narrowed at the center of his big head. "Excuse me? Seriously, if we must do it, then we might as well enjoy." I saw a shimmer of excitement come across his face.

"First things first. First, I am in charge here. Give me your purse and keys." I walked over, picked up my purse and my big key chain. He threw my keys and everything in my purse into a small safe on the dresser. I neatly laid my jeans, shirt, and shoes on the chair.

"Not so fast; let me see your jeans." I handed them over and he searched the pockets. "Okay. Now we can have FUN," he grinned. I gritted my teeth. *Yes, we can.*

This man was about twenty years older than me and not in shape at all. We had sex and he fell asleep, his arm on me as before, but thankfully no gun. Around ten I woke him up. "Round two," I smiled, and we had sex again. This time he passed out hard. I turned on the TV that had inches of dust on it. The picture you couldn't make out, but the noise was nice since it drowned out the sleeping snoring monster. I wanted to see how sound asleep he was, so I lifted his arm and slipped underneath it. He grumbled but didn't wake up.

Deep breath I told myself. I slid off the bed and went into the bathroom; he still didn't move. Okay. God, I whispered, *please protect me.* I walked over and started to get dressed. Every part of my body was shaking uncontrollably. I leaned over to pick up my tennis shoes that had my spare key taped on the bottom. My fingers trembled as I slowly turned the knob. He didn't move. I slowly closed the door behind me.

By the time I got to my car I was so sick to my stomach I wanted to vomit everywhere. I was breathing heavily and trembled as I pulled the key off my shoe. I looked all around me to make sure I was alone and shook with fear as I turned the lock to open my car door. I slid in, still watching the motel door, praying it wouldn't open. As I started my car I made sure my lights stayed off. When I pulled onto the highway my heart was about to pump out of my chest. My fingertips were white as they gripped the steering wheel.

On my drive to Bobby and Gail's, I prayed. "Please God, make a way." I was crying so hard I couldn't breathe. I pulled in to Bobby and Gail's around midnight but was shocked by what I saw. Their place was lit up like the fourth of July and a huge U-Haul truck was in the driveway. I parked my car and rubbed my face to try to hide the mascara streaks. I peeked inside the U-Haul and gasped as I saw it was loaded down with everything, including appliances and all their furniture. What in the world was going on?

I walked in to see Bobby and Gail hovered over the table studying a map. "What's up?" I asked, walking over to where they were. They both jumped when they heard my voice.

"Oh! We didn't know you were staying over tonight."

I lowered my head. "Sorry, I should have called."

"Have you been crying?" Gail sweetly touched my face.

"Boy problems." I shrugged my shoulders.

"Oh," she shook her head and hugged me tighter. "This will pass." She patted my back.

"Like a kidney stone," I mumbled.

"Gail, no time to waste. Jody, we're leaving," Bobby said, still studying the map.

"When?" I asked.

"As soon as we get everything packed up." Gail walked over and put her arm around me. "You have been the best nanny and we will miss you so much." Her eyes started to water.

"Where are you going?" I jumped back, my heart rushing. *No this isn't happening. My whole world is falling around me.* I started to tremble and cry.

"OMG, are you okay?"

"No, Gail, I am not. I can't breathe."

Gail walked over with a paper bag. "Breathe into this, sweetie." As she held my hand, she explained, "We need to go."

"Why in the middle of the night?"

"Fewer questions…" chimed in Bobby.

"Where?" I asked again.

"We're closing our eyes and picking the place." Gail handed me a tissue and I blew my nose. "Jody, we didn't think of this before, but do you want to go with us?" Gail hugged me even tighter.

"Really?" I pulled the paper bag away from my mouth.

"Really," Gail smiled. "The children love you." She smiled softly at me. "We must leave tonight, and I am sure your parents are sound asleep."

I nodded my head up and down. "Yes, but I am eighteen now. I need to go to the bathroom." I leaned over the sink and stared at the hot mess looking back at me. I am lucky to be alive. *God, is this my way out?* My mind flashed back to the terror I had been through twice now. When he wakes up and I am not there, he is coming for me full force. I started to run the cold water and splashed my face. What do you do? They knew everything about me and my life. I was a rebelling teenager Trek had listened to, and now my whole life had become a living nightmare. I couldn't escape. I prayed so hard, "Please God, forgive me for putting my family in the way of evil. Please, God, help me. I trust you, God, that you will protect them. Please, God, give me a sign they will not be harmed or killed by these evil people if I leave."

I stepped outside to the U-Haul and saw a star shoot across the sky. God had answered my prayer, I felt peace. I had prayed for and God just gave me my way out.

*****

If you are reading this, let it be a warning: be careful with whom you trust your life's information. I trusted Trek with mine, and I didn't even know him. I took the bait of his lies and deception as he promised me the world. It took me years to put the pieces together that I escaped human trafficking. That was the plan for me and I had no idea. The devil doesn't come as a red man with a pointed tail and horns. The devil will disguise himself as everything you have ever wanted. It is not your fault.

If you are also a victim of someone hurting you, please know you are not alone. Twelve-Step Recovery groups are there to help you. God does love you. There is a purpose in the pain. Please don't blame yourself; it is never your fault. I lived with guilt for years. The best thing I ever did was give it all to God.

Chapter Five

RUNNING SCARED

Bobby was in front of us as Gail drove the big 1970 bright yellow Cadillac. I looked out the window at the trees passing in the darkness. "You seem to be miles away." Gail raised an eyebrow.

"Rough day."

"Well, lie back and get some rest; it's going to be a long ride."

"Oh yeah," I laughed. "Where are we going?"

"Where Mickey Mouse lives." She patted my leg. "It's a long drive, so try to get some rest."

I laid my head back on the headrest. "Hey, Gail, can we please pull over? I want to call my mom."

"When we stop for gas in about 2 hours you can."

"On second thought, I don't want to wake my dad. I will call after sunrise."

We drove for hours, the kids sleeping most of the way. We did have a flat tire on the U-Haul from too much weight and had to wait for it to be fixed at a gas station in the middle of nowhere. I couldn't put it off anymore. I needed to call my mom.

I walked over to a payphone and punched in my parents' phone number. My mom picked up on the third ring. A professional-sounding voice said, "Hello. Will you accept this collect call from…"

I blurted in before she could finish. "Mom, it's me."

"Yes," she replied. I could feel her confusion through the phone.

"Hi, Mommy."

"Jody, why are you calling me collect? Are you okay?"

"No, Mom, I'm not. Mom, I messed up really bad," the tears started to fall.

"Are you in trouble, baby?" She pleaded with me for answers.

"Mom, I can't say much but I am safe. I am with Bobby and Gail in another state."

"WHAT? They moved?"

"Yes. Mom, please, not a word to anyone. Promise me, please!"

I heard my mom sniffle and it ripped out my heart. "OK, sweetheart. Where do I tell people you are?"

"Out of the country on a last-minute mission trip. If anyone calls, Mom, please tell them that!"

"You must enter ten cents to continue your call."

"I must go. I love you so much, Mom."

"Jody, where are you going?

"I can't, Mom. I just can't tell you anymore. I must go now. I love you. Tell Daddy, Melinda and Melissa I love them too. Thank you, Mom. I love you. Bye for now." I hung up the phone and cried like a baby. *Please God, please protect my family.*

And God did. Years later, I told my sister what happened. She said some guy with a deep voice called the house like twenty times. Dad finally yelled at him, and he didn't call again. Someone also was riding slowly by the house. Dad sat on the front porch with his shotgun and that stopped too. I thanked God for the hedge of protection over my family. Prayer really does work.

We arrived in Florida. The salt air and beautiful beach was exactly what I needed. It was weird because Bobby and Gail lived in a small house and had a beat-up car but were spending some money in Florida. *Have they hit the lottery?* I wondered.

They rented this big two-story brick house with a two-car garage. WOW. I clapped my hands in excitement. Gail beamed at me. "I always wanted a beautiful home like this." We all piled out of the car and ran through the house.

"This is my room." Each kid claimed his or her space.

"Jody, it means so much that you moved with us; this is your room." Gail opened the door to a beautiful room.

"Wow," I gasped.

"I know," she smiled at me. "Hopefully, this will help you forget about that jerk back home."

I sat on the floor of the empty bedroom. "Can I have a minute, please?"

"Sure," Gail smiled as she closed my door. I got on my knees and, hands folded, began to pray. "Thank you, Jesus. Thank you." I cried harder thinking of the last 48 hours.

The house we got was now home, and the kids loved it. Bobby and Gail were in heaven occupying the only bedroom on the bottom floor. "We will block off the stairs at night."

"No problem," I smiled. "I will make sure the kids are okay." Gail smiled as she patted Bobby on the butt. They playfully rushed off into their new room.

I wanted to help pay for my stay and not just babysitting. I got two jobs right away - one working at a cable company, eight to five and on weekends, and a night job working as a hostess at a restaurant on the water. This place had the best coconut shrimp and the manager would sneak me a few from time to time. I thought everything was finally going well. It had been a week and I wanted to call my mom.

"Hi, Mom."

"Jody, where are you?" The concern was back in her voice.

I paused. "I can't say."

I was keeping a secret from my mom, and little did I know Bobby and Gail were keeping a big secret of their own…

Secrets Revealed

Bobby and Gail had filled the rental house with all kinds of nice furniture. Our house looked like something out of a Southern Living magazine. The living room had couches and recliners for adults and the kids.

"How cute," I laughed at the mini recliners.

"I just fell in love with them," Gail giggled back.

"You are very good at decorating," I smiled.

"Wait till you see your room," she winked.

"WHAT?" I ran up the stairs as fast as I could. When I opened the door I saw the dresser, the nightstand, the sleigh bed all matched in a gorgeous dark cherry wood. "WOW!" My eyes bugged out of my head. "I don't know what to say. It's so gorgeous."

Gail strolled across the room to switch on my new crystal lamp. "It's a thank you for everything you have done for us."

I grabbed her close and hugged her tight. "No Gail, thank you."

Life was good. We had been settled in a little over four months. I

Running Scared

talked to my mom a few times, still not saying where I was, but that I was safe. I felt like the worst daughter on the planet. Work was going great at the cable company. I had made good friends with Macey, a feisty redhead with a body that would stop traffic. Her boyfriend Dustin was goofy but also built like a Mack truck. They were doing contract work at the office.

One day, a man walked in looking like a carrot-top John Candy, but with more freckles. "May I help you?"

Macey giggled. "Dustin and I work for him; this is Robbie."

"Well, hello beautiful," he said, taking my hand and kissing it softly. *Barf* I thought. *Who is this red-headed Romeo?* "Can I take you out to dinner?" He looked up and locked eyes with me.

"I don't know," I replied snatching back by hand. The last thing I wanted was to be around a strange guy. I was so scared of being alone with any guy. I didn't see them as just guys; I saw them as hungry wolves seeking out the next meal.

"Let's all go. I am starved!" Macey shouted.

"Me too," Dustin rubbed is stomach.

Having Macey and Dustin with me gave me comfort, so I agreed to go. "Only for a little while," I whispered to Macey.

She rolled her eyes. "Okay, Grandma!"

We pulled up to the valet stand at the restaurant. "Fancy Pants, as usual." Macey patted Robbie on his back.

"Only the best for my employees." He handed his keys to the valet. "Take care of my baby – no scratches."

"Yes, Sir." I am sure the valet guy wanted to take that key and run it all the way down Mr. Fancy Pants' truck.

We walked into the restaurant that had gorgeous chandeliers

hanging from the ceiling and white tablecloths covering the tables. "Reservation?" the hostess asked.

"Robbie, party of four." *Hmm party of four, huh. Someone had planned this.*

"Would you like a drink?" Robbie grinned over the drink menu.

"I'm only eighteen," I replied.

He smiled. "I didn't ask you your age. I asked if I could buy you a drink."

"No, thank you," I replied.

"Looks like we got us a Sandra Dee." Macey sipped her red wine.

"Not exactly," I shrugged my shoulders. Dinner was good, and conversation flowed nicely. I really wanted to get home, put on my jammies and crawl into my new comfy bed. I wasn't comfortable around people. I wondered who was watching me. Was I being followed? "This has been nice, but can you please take me back to my car?"

"Sure," Robbie chugged the last of his red wine.

"What? It's early," Macey hiccupped.

"Work tomorrow." I replied.

When I got back to Bobby and Gail's the energy in the room was different. "Is everything okay?" I asked.

"Yes, of course," Gail said. I could tell that Gail's eyes were swollen from crying. She sat in a ball with her knees up on the coach. She rocked back and forth. The kids were running around crazy and she sat there in a daze.

"I will take the kids upstairs to play."

Gail nodded her head. "Yes, please." I had never seen Gail like this before. I wondered if someone had died in the family.

"Can I get you anything?" I leaned over to give her a hug.

"Watching the kids is so helpful, sweetie. I don't want them to see me upset." As I walked up the stairs I heard Bobby come in and slam the door behind him. I had no idea what was happening, but I knew they were fighting about something. I took the kids upstairs to play. That was my favorite thing to do anyway. I could tell the conversation between Bobby and Gail was getting louder, so I closed the door and turned up the TV.

The next day, no one was home when I got off work. Gail had left a note on the counter. "Family outing, be back this afternoon. Have a great day at work. Love, Gail." I breathed a sigh of relief – they made up. I poured my coffee, got dressed and was out the door. Macey, who picked me up, honked the horn. "Come on, slow poke." She was a bit crazy, but I was thankful for her friendship.

I had been at work for a few hours when I got the phone call I never thought I would get from Gail. I answered and heard Gail's voice. "Jody?" She was crying so hard into the phone.

"Gail, are you okay? Are the kids okay?" I couldn't make out her words she was crying so hard.

"Jody, we haven't been honest with you."

"What?" My heart sank. "Gail?" My heart started to beat out of my chest. "Gail, please."

"Jody, we're running from the law, and we must keep running. Bobby was stealing not only items from Plump Pal, but also embezzling checks. We have bounced a lot of checks."

Now my heart raced. "What?"

The room started spinning around me. I couldn't breathe. I couldn't comprehend what I was hearing. "Gail…"

"Jody, we're sorry, but we must go. We have already packed up our things."

"What about all the furniture?" I started to rock back and forth in my chair, tears rolling down my face.

"It's at the house, I am sure they will repo once they figure out the checks are bad."

I can't breathe. "GAIL!"

"We must go now, and you can't come with us. We do love you Jody, I am so sorry." My body went limp and I felt like I was going to pass out.

"Gail, please take me!"

"I can't sweetheart…"

My heart dropped. "PLEASE?" I cried. Then the phone went dead.

Chapter Six

RUNNING INTO ROBBIE

I sat there, tears streaming down my face. "What's wrong?" Macey asked.

"Everything," I replied. "Can you please watch the phone? I need to go the restroom." Everything around me was spinning like a top. I stood up and had to grab my desk to keep from falling to the floor. *What do I do? Where do I go?* I saw the big black wolf from the motel in my mind circling me again. *I can't escape my life.* I finally got strength enough to leave my reception desk and walked as fast as I could into the restroom. My mind began to race. *I can't move home! He is going to find me.*

I pushed through the bathroom stall just in time before I vomited. I lay down on the cold floor. Then I threw up again. Macey walked in. "What the heck is wrong with you?"

"Nothing, really," I replied.

Really? Because you sure look pregnant to me." Her hands were on her hips as she laughed.

"DON'T SAY THAT!" The thought made me turn and throw up again. "I think I have a stomach bug."

"Liar," she joked.

Then, like diarrhea, the words started coming out about Bobby and Gail and how I was stuck with nowhere to go.

"WOW!" Macey sat down beside me. "Can't you just go home?"

"NO!" I shook my head. "That's not an option."

"Oh," Macey handed me a wet paper towel. Suddenly her face looked like the Cheshire cat on "Alice In Wonderland."

I leaned up. "What is it?"

"You know Robbie has a crush on you, right?"

Ugh, the red-haired boss who fell out of the ugly tree and hit every branch on the way down, I thought. "Really?" I decided to act interested. *Bless my heart.* What choice did I have? I had hit an all-time low as this toilet bowl was my new best friend.

"Who is answering the phone? Our boss is pissed as a wet cat."

"Oh, sorry, that's me." Macey hurriedly shut the bathroom stall so Miss Pissy Pants didn't see me.

"What are you doing in there?" She cocked up an eyebrow.

"Jody has a stomach bug." Macey covered her mouth.

"I feel better now," I spoke up. "I think I just ate some bad food. I can go back to my desk."

Macey came over, still all smiles. "Sooo, what do you think about Robbie?" She leaned back as if she was daydreaming. "I hate being the ONLY girl traveling with two dudes." She turned and pointed to me, "but if you date Robbie you can travel with us."

I started to rub my temples with my fingertips. "How old is he exactly?"

Macey wrinkled up her face. "Well…33."

"I am 18." I looked off in the distance to think. My mind began to race. *You have no education. No one will hire you. You are dirty.*

No one will date you. You are running. You better keep running, or the wolf and his pack will find you.

"I would love to go out with him," I blurted. At this point, I didn't feel I had a choice.

Laughing, Macey said, "Well, good. Don't worry about a place to stay either. You can stay with us rent free," she winked. "We travel a lot, so get ready to see the world."

Travel sounded so good to me; the less I stay in one place the better. "Thank you," I replied. Relief flooded through me. Survived one more obstacle thrown at me.

"After work we will go get your stuff. Do we need Robbie's truck?" Her eyes were big with excitement.

"I don't need a truck." I thought, *all the furniture is stolen.* "Your car is fine, Macey."

It's crazy how one minute the ride is calm like the ocean, and the next it is rough with huge waves. As I walked into the house that once held so much happiness, it now felt heavy and empty. My eyes stung as the tears started to roll down my face. I could no longer stand and I fell to my knees. Macey walked over and put her arm around me.

"Jody, look at me." I looked up at this red-headed beauty who now had tears in her green eyes. "It's going to be okay."

"I…I don't even know you guys, Macey." I couldn't breathe as waterfalls of tears fell down my snotty face.

"We are your family now." She leaned over and kissed my forehead. "Robbie will take good care of you, just like he has us. Leave this in your past."

We got all my clothes, and as I walked out the door, I whispered.

"Thank you, Bobby and Gail. You don't know it, but you saved my life." And I closed and locked the door.

*****

We were driving along the coast and the water was so peaceful. We came to a big gate and Macey reached out the window to put in her code. "This is home for now," she grinned over her shoulder at me. Stately palm trees were along the driveway and then I saw this huge condo.

"You live in a condo?"

"Not just a condo," she smiled. "The penthouse."

"Seriously?" I shook my head, again shocked at my life. *One-minute poor as a church mouse, the next in a penthouse* I whispered.

Macey grabbed my hand. "Only the best for Robbie, but everywhere we stay is temporary. We move a lot with work."

"I can do temporary," I smiled back. As we went up the elevator my ears started to pop. This was the highest above the earth I had ever been. We walked out onto very colorful carpet.

"This carpet is hideous," I laughed.

"That's because rich people don't look down." She winked at me. As we opened the door to beautiful marble flooring my mouth flew open. "I know, right?" Macey giggled. "We have company," she announced.

I gave her a look like *OMG you didn't tell him?*

"Welcome." Robbie was chilling on the couch with Dustin.

"WOW!" I gasped at the view behind him. It was like nothing I had ever seen. The water was so blue and huge boats filled it like a bathtub with rubber duckies.

"Oh yeah." Robbie smiled. "Welcome to Paradise."

I swallowed hard. "Thank you."

"We will put you in the guest room." Macey picked up my bags.

"Sorry about the trash bags," I blushed.

Robbie sat up. "So, I take it this is a longer stay than a sleepover?"

Macey chimed in. "Robbie, she is homeless. The people she nannied for left her in Florida, ALONE." She tapped her foot in frustration. "Be nice."

As we walked into my guest room I asked Macey, "You can talk to your boss like that?"

"Oh, he is more like a brother than a boss," she grinned. "When Dustin and I moved from Texas we both needed to find a place to live and work fast. There was an ad in the paper and we met Robbie. We have been traveling with him for over three years. Living together you really do become family."

I walked over to my window. "Everything seems so small up here. I feel like I am safe." I was so far away from everything evil below me. I thanked God again for a place to stay.

"The safest." Macey walked over beside me, "and we are going to be the best of friends." I stayed in my room alone most of the night. I felt weird being in the living room like I was intruding. The less they see me, the less bothersome I will be. I slept so well that night. I couldn't believe it, but this bed was more comfortable than my last one.

A month had passed, and I became more and more comfortable around my new family. I was thankful that Robbie respected my space, that I had just got out of a bad relationship and needed to take things slowly. He was very understanding.

One morning about a month later I woke up and Macey was

sitting next to me with a mug of coffee. "Good morning, Sunshine," she said with a big smile on her face.

I sat up to pull my eye mask off and was blinded by the sun streaming through my bedroom window. "Good morning," I growled.

"Got some news," she blurted and took a sip of her coffee.

"What's that?" I asked. I am not a morning person so news before coffee is never good.

"We're moving." She peered over her mug.

Sadness filled me. I looked out the window at the water that sparkled like diamonds. "Where?" I shook my head to try and wake up.

"Hot Lanta." She stood up and started to shake her booty.

"Too early for that, Macey." I rolled my eyes at her.

Then Macey's boyfriend, Dustin, walked in, his hair a mess. "Did you tell her?" he asked. His eyes darted back and forth between Macey and me.

She nodded and smiled, nodding her head yes.

"I didn't say I was going." I lay back on my pillow.

"Duh, you are." Macey grabbed a pillow and smacked me with it.

"Can I finish my coffee, please?" I pushed her off my bed.

"Sure thing but get ready because we are going to be some sweet Georgia peaches."

Life was so simple for Macey. She was on this huge vacation where she traveled and got excited about each new place. She was running for fun, I was running for my life. I lay back and looked at the freshly painted ceiling. *What if my picture was out there? What if they were all looking for me?* Fear covered me, and my body trembled at the thought. *He is out there roaming, looking for me. I have nowhere to stay here.* I knew I had to go.

I called my mom to tell her. "Hello? Mom?"

"Jody, how are you?" I could hear the relief in her voice. "Jody I am worried sick about you. Where are you?"

"It doesn't matter, Mom."

"Why not?"

"I'm moving."

"Again? Jody! What is going on with you? Promise me you are okay?"

"Yes, I promise, Mom." Here came the waterworks again. I missed my family so much and couldn't hold back the tears. "Has anyone called for me?" I held my breath for an answer.

"No," my mom replied. My body relaxed. "Jody?"

"Yes, Mom?"

"Where are you moving?"

"I can't tell you," I sobbed. "I am so sorry, Mom, for everything."

"It's okay, baby. I am just so worried about you."

"Just pray for me, Mom."

"I always do, baby girl."

We said, "I love you" and "Goodbye" and hung up.

It didn't take us long to pack. The next morning, I woke up to find a huge suitcase with a big red bow. I walked out to the kitchen area where Robbie was sitting at the bar having coffee.

"Did you get my present?" He turned and gave me a huge freckled-face smile. It was then I noticed how much Macey and he looked alike. Well.... the red hair parts.

"Oh, sorry, yes thank you."

"Looks much better than black trash bags, don't you agree?"

I shrugged with a half-smile. "It does."

The next morning, we packed up Macey's car and Robbie's truck and headed away from the beautiful condo to Atlanta.

Trauma Triggers

When something like this happens to you, you have trauma triggers. It could be a smell, sound, song, place, car, and the list will go on. That one trigger will take you back to when the trauma happened.

A big black man raped me, so of course, that was a trigger for me. Any older big black man I would panic, but a good-looking white man lured me in, and that was an even bigger trigger. As you already figured out, "men" were a trigger, all men.

I was petrified to be around men.

*****

"You should ride with Robbie," Macey smirked, putting the last bag in her car.

I opened the door of Robbie's truck and froze where I stood. All the color drained from my face. Memories flooded from the last time I opened a door to a man looking back at me. Robbie patted the seat. "Hop in," he smiled.

"I can't. I feel sick." Robbie looked at me confused. "I am a good driver."

I backed away and shut the door. Hands shaking, I walked over to Macey's car. "Dustin, can I please ride with Macey and you with Robbie?"

Dustin hopped out of Macey's car. "Football talk over makeup? Heck yeah!"

"Thank you." I crawled in the seat next to Macey. I rubbed my hands together to keep her from seeing them shake. "Girl time," I smiled. We talked about every kind of fashion there was, makeup, boyfriends, and I wanted so bad to tell her about Trek, but I shook that thought off.

"So, Robbie really does have a thing for you."

I rolled my eyes and stared out the window. "You know you and Robbie look a lot alike."

"What? That's crazy. We both have red hair yes, but I have way better bone structure."

I shook my head. "Is he your real brother?"

"No, he is like a brother, but my real brother lives in Texas and he is good looking like me." She flipped her hair. "Back to my subject – what do you think about Robbie?"

I shrugged my shoulders. "He is growing on me. One day at a time."

The next day we pulled up at this beautiful home on a golf course in Atlanta, also in a gated community. I thanked God for the extra protection. Having a gate made me feel safe. The wolf can pace back and forth but not get in. "Wow! Is this our house?" Macey gasped and shook me from my thoughts. I looked out the front windshield at a two-story home with big picture windows and three big white columns lining the front.

"It must be." I smiled. Wow! Robbie made a good living with the contracting company he owned. I wondered how much this one cost to rent.

As we got out of the car Robbie walked over to me. "We are working from home here, so the good news is you get the biggest bedroom in the house; the bad news is it's with me."

There it is – another punch to my gut. I forced a big smile. "Sounds like a plan to me." We walked into the front door of the house with huge cathedral ceilings, a crystal chandelier and the most gorgeous iron staircase.

"I love houses move-in ready," Robbie said, chest poked out and proud.

"It is lovely." I nodded my head in agreement.

"Shall we check out our room?"

"Yes, please lead the way."

"Well, I am not sure where," he smiled, "but it is on the bottom floor. Let's find it together." And he bent his arm for me to grab it like we were walking into a fancy party.

I know why they call it a master bedroom. This one room was bigger than my sisters' and my room put together. I no longer had a view of the water, but a gorgeous view of green grass and golfers in funny outfits with worse shoes. A huge iron canopy bed sat in the center with night stands on each side. A bench sat at the end of the bed. *I am not quite sure why you need a bench if you have a bed to sit on.* A huge picture window with two unique sitting chairs.

"Why do they need so much sitting area in here?" I turned to Robbie.

"You really are a country girl." He shook his head. "To fill up the room so it looks nice." He winked. "Are you ready for the best part?"

"Sure!" He opened these double doors to the biggest bathroom I had ever seen.

"Wow." Marble lined the floor and there were two sides with two sinks. My side had a huge mirror with a vanity area to sit at. "I feel like Goldie Hawn in 'Overboard.'" I smiled at Robbie.

"Oh, we are not done." He smiled and walked over to a door on my side of the bathroom. My eyes about popped out of my head when I saw this huge walk-in closet. "A closet you can walk into."

I walked in and took a deep breath to take in everything around me. "We can fill it up later." Robbie grinned at me. *He really is a great guy I thought. He is way older than me, but he is a good guy. He took me in and he didn't have too. He made sure I had a roof over my head and food in my stomach.* I started to see him in a different light.

Macey walked into the bedroom carrying a box and wearing a big smile. "Not bad, huh?"

"Not at all," I whispered back.

"OMG! Check out this bathroom and closet. Too bad it's super empty." Macey laughed.

"I know." I lowered my head, embarrassed. I hardly had any clothes because of how much I'd been running. It's not like I could take a wardrobe with me everywhere I went.

As promised, Robbie came out and handed us his credit card. "Time to fill up that big closet."

"I can't," I shook my head.

"Jody, you need clothes and I can write it off." He winked at me. "You are now employed by me."

"I am?" My eyes widened.

"Yes, I am going to get you set up in a home office, answering phones."

"OK," I smiled. "I would like that."

Macey grabbed the credit card. "All this boring talk – let's go shopping." She grabbed my hand and headed out the door.

When we were in her car, I asked, "Do you think Robbie will let me stay if I don't sleep with him?"

"What?" She slammed on the brakes and the car behind us almost hit us. "Where is that coming from?"

"That car almost hit us!"

"Well, I wasn't expecting that!" Macey looked at me like I was crazy. "Where did that come from?"

"Well," I started to fumble my fingers, not knowing exactly how to reply.

She turned quickly to me and said, "OMG, Jo Jo, are you a virgin?"

The word VIRGIN shot through me like fire. I wanted to say YES! *I have been saving myself for that special one.* That wasn't the case; I had been robbed of that dream.

"Kinda," I said slowly.

"Kinda," she laughed. "There is no *kinda*." She had no idea what I meant.

"I will say this. Robbie can get any woman he wants, and girl, he wants you."

"I thought so," I said back.

"Really?" Macey laughed. "Jody the guy is crazy about you. He has been patient. That is an understatement. He knows you are young and he respects you."

Respects me? The thought was comical to me. If only he knew just how dirty I was. If he knew where I had been. They would kick me out so fast, out on the streets where I belonged. "I just think Robbie is going to get tired of me." My eyes teared up.

"You are always so darn serious, woman. I don't think he is," she said. "This is a fun day, let's shop!"

"Wait, Macey. Can I tell you something private?" It was the first time I ever saw her big smile turn serious.

"Of course, Jo Jo."

This is it. I am going to share with someone what happened to me. I am going to finally say the words out loud. I took a deep breath to prepare myself. Then just like a waterfall, the thoughts flooded my mind. *You are not worthy. She will tell Robbie. He will think you are disgusting. He will never want someone else's trash. He is going to see just how stupid you are! Stoooop,* screamed in my head.

"Never mind," I said.

"Tell me," pleaded Macey. "I am not letting you off that easy, young lady. What is it?"

"I am a virgin," the words slipped out before I could stop them.

"I knew it," she smiled. "No one is "kinda" a virgin, girl. Once you have sex, you will understand." Little did she know I clearly understood what sex was.

As we walked into the shopping mall, Macey was all smiles and ready to shop. I was so full of fear, though, that I could barely move. *Is he here? Is Trek here? What if we were followed? What if he is waiting in the parking lot?* Flashes of the gun and being kidnapped again flashed in my mind. Fear flooded over me again. The huge mall began to close in on me. Every person who passed by made me wonder if they knew him. H*e is going to find me and kill me. Kill me. OMG, I can't breathe. I need to talk to my mom. My family.*

I told Macey I would be right back and ran through the mall looking for a payphone. You have no idea the fear that takes over when you think your family could die at any minute. Here I am living in this huge house in a fairyland that didn't exist. I was running. Running and scared. I finally found a pay phone. It had been a few weeks since I had called home.

My fingers shook as I dialed the phone. "Will you accept a collect call from… "Mom, it's me."

"Yes, I will."

"Mommy!"

My heart swelled just hearing her voice. *Thank you, Jesus. My family is okay.* "Hi Mom. I'm good. We moved into this big beautiful house on a golf course."

"Who is we?"

"Some friends I met in Florida. They are really good people. They are taking good care of me."

"Oh, okay. Jody, this little town is buzzing like crazy. Did you know Bobby and Gail were running from the law?" The phone went silent.

"No, Mom, I promise I didn't know when we left. I found out a few days ago. We split up."

"Jody, are you running from the law?" Her voice was not one of accusation but of concern.

I wanted to scream, *No, worse! Mommy I was raped, and he threatened to kill all of you!* But I just replied, "No, Mom. I'm just trying to figure out my place in life. I promise you I am very safe, Mom." I couldn't tell her the truth. I didn't want her to worry but I knew she did.

"Praying for you, baby." The sound of her voice hurt my heart so bad. The guilt and shame covered me like a wet blanket.

"Mom?"

"Yes, baby."

"Has anyone called for me since we last spoke?"

"No baby, why? Are you expecting someone to call?"

"Just curious. I love you, Mom."

"I love you, too, baby. Jody?"

"Yes, Mom."

"I miss you so much."

"I miss you more, Mom."

I hung up the phone and tears streamed down my face. *My family was okay. He had stopped calling. It had only been months. Was the nightmare over? Did he believe I moved out of the country?*

In the middle of my thoughts, Macey came charging at me like a bull in a china shop. "Jo Jo, let's shop. I didn't bring you to the mall to stay on a pay phone. They have the cutest shoes over here." She knew shoes were my weakness. Shoes made me smile no matter what.

We came back with tons of shopping bags. Macey floated up the stairs to her room, and I slowly crawled up to "our" room. I must admit it was nice having this huge bedroom and walk-in closet to fill up, but I wasn't happy. I was just living day by day.

We all hung out and watched TV on the big leather couches. This was the biggest TV I had ever seen. Sitting around with them made me think back to when my family always sat together and watched TV. I held back the tears. *I must quit crying so much around them.* Macey let out a big yawn. "Well, Ladies and Gents, I do believe it is time for this chick to go to bed."

"We can stay up a little later." I pulled her back down on the couch.

"No." She stood back up. "Dustin wants to 'read' to me. Don't you

Dustin?" Dustin was cute, but not the smartest.

"Not really, Macey. I would rather watch TV than read." Macey reached over and whispered something in Dustin's ear. He jumped up, stretching. "Oh, I just got so tired." Macey giggled as Dustin chased her into the bedroom.

Robbie looked at me and I felt like the whole room was on fire. "Are you tired?"

"Not at all," I said. "I am a night owl." He clicked the TV off and my heart raced.

"Big day tomorrow, let's go to bed." I went into my closet and put on flannel pants and a big flannel shirt. I walked into the bedroom and Robbie started to laugh. "You are always full of surprises, Miss Jody. You do know it's June." He raised an eyebrow. Lying in the big bed, he motioned me over.

"Robbie," I stopped before climbing in. "I am just not comfortable. I'm sorry. I'm going to watch some more TV in the living room." I walked over and kissed him on the cheek. "Thank you for being so kind to me."

I made me a pallet on the couch – the kind my mom used to make me when I was sick. My eyes got heavy and I fell asleep. In the middle of the night, someone touched my arm. I jump up swinging and screaming, "Don't touch me."

"Jody, calm down. It's me, Robbie."

"Don't touch me," I snapped. I thought he was going to rape me.

"Jody, I think you had a bad dream," he smiled. "You know I won't hurt you. I have this huge bed, and you're on this small couch."

"I am fine. Thank you." I pulled the covers up around my neck.

"I will make you a deal." He smiled at me.

"Okay. I'm listening."

"I will put a pillow in the middle of the bed. I promise not to come on your side. I just can't have you sleeping out here like we are in a fight or something." His eyes looked sincere. "Trust me, Jody."

I lay in that bed, my mind racing. My body stayed so tense, I didn't want to move. Every second that went by, I wondered if he was going to hurt me. My knees locked, and that is how I finally went to sleep. When the sun came up, I looked around the big fancy bedroom. *Life is crazy,* I thought. A month ago, I woke up in the most disgusting motel ever. I thanked God I was alive.

While still in bed, I heard a loud horn outside the window. I looked out, and there was a beautiful RV pulling into the driveway. *Who the heck is this?*

I quickly got dressed and flew down the stairs to find coffee. I got myself a cup and went outside where everyone was standing.

"Good morning," I said.

"Well, good morning, sleepy head." Robbie smiled.

"You know me," I smiled back.

"What's this?"

Macey was right behind me. She started to do the "happy dance" that looked like a bad MC Hammer move. I need more coffee, I thought

"Saddle up, girlfriend, we are headed to Kentucky."

My eyes popped out of my head. I slapped my hand to my forehead. "Are we moving again? I just got settled in." The frustration started to build as I paced back and forth.

"No, silly," Macey laughed. "This is our ride to the horse races!"

"The horse races? This is the first time I heard about horse races."

"Oh, yeah," Macey replied. "Robbie is huge into horse races. The man likes to gamble."

"You have been before?" All I could think *was is this a trick? Did they bait me in and now they are taking me back in this RV?* MY head started to spin. I need to sit down. I was overwhelmed by everything going on.

Macey came over and sat down beside me. "It's going to be the best weekend ever! Don't be upset, Jody. You are going to love the horse races!" Robbie and Dustin walked over to where we sat.

Robbie looked at me. "You can stay at the house if you don't want to go."

My insides screamed to *please not leave me alone in the huge house.* The thought of it sent shivers down my spine. I did feel some relief if he offered for me to stay home, then it must really be the horse races. "Hmm," I said.

"No, Robbie!" Macey smacked his leg. "I need my girl to go!"

"I would love to go." I smiled.

"Yea!" Macey hugged me so hard we fell backwards laughing.

"When are we going?"

"Thursday to Thursday." Macey beamed at me.

It seemed like the week flew by. Before I knew it, it was Thursday and time to leave. I stood in my oversized closet trying to figure out what to bring. Macey came in. "Are you staying in there all night?" She flipped the closet light off and on.

"Sorry." I fumbled through my shirts. "I don't know what to bring."

"Clothes," she giggled. "Unless you want to run around naked with the horses." I rolled my eyes. "Have you ever been camping?"

Macey started to try on my boots.

"Yes." I handed her the other one.

"Well, think of it as camping, but no paved lots, just dirt."

"Macey!"

"Sorry, that's the best I can do," as she pranced off in my boots.

I packed the best I could and walked out to the RV. Looking up at the night sky it reminded me of packing up the U-Haul to leave with Bobby and Gail. I wondered where they were and if the kids were okay.

"You can sit co-pilot." Robbie walked up and put a hat on my head.

"Thanks," I laughed. I fidgeted in my seat as we drove deeper into the woods. "Where are we?" I asked. I seemed hours had passed.

"Back roads, less traffic." Robbie grinned.

"We are almost there," Macey piped up from the back.

When we pulled up to the racetrack, it was very dusty and campers were everywhere. I breathed a sigh of relief. We must have been VIP because we had the best spot to park in the middle of the track. "WOW! We are parking here?"

"Only the best parking lot," Macey said, as she opened the RV door, coughing at the dust and waving her hands to try and get rid of it. The track had lights all the way around it and people were sitting outside their campers drinking beer. Off-the-track cabins were lined up in a row and there was a big lake and even more campers. Those campers had campfires going. I secretly wanted to park over there.

"Robbie," I whispered.

"Yeah, what's up?"

"I know this is a prime spot, but do you think we could move closer to the lake? It reminds me of camping as a kid."

"Yes, please," chimed in Macey, "and less dust too."

Robbie leaned over and whispered in my ear. "I'll see what I can do; be right back." He came walking back a few minutes later like a proud peacock. He shut the RV door. "I got good news." He gave me a big smile.

"Yea!" I felt happy. Happy, wow I hadn't felt that way in a long time. Being near that water made me happy. We pulled into the perfect slot right by the lake but not far from the track.

"Are you sure you're okay here?" I asked.

"If you're happy, I'm happy." Robbie smiled back.

"Thank you," and I gave him the biggest hug.

As we were unloading, this skinny guy came walking up, *He's so skinny, if he stood sideways and stuck out his tongue, he'd look like a zipper.* I thought.

Jerking his head from side to side. He was maybe four feet tall and weighed ninety pounds, if that. "Well, lookie here. Big Robbie ain't in the middle of the track."

Macey rolled her eyes. "This is Fast Jack." The little man held out his hand. "At your service." I shook his hand quickly and pulled it away. This guy creeped me out more than normal. He had bloodshot eyes and sniffed a lot. He talked super-fast. "Where you from? You like to camp? You do? You don't?" Even I couldn't keep up with this guy.

Robbie came around the side of the RV. "Wow, big man, can't believe you're slumming it over here and not in VIP."

"You worry about winning me some money and not where I park my RV. You ready to win me big money?"

"Always." replied Fast Jack. Robbie walked back into the RV and left me standing there with Fast Jack. His creepy eyes fell on me and ran up and down from the top of my head to my toes. "You like riding big horses?"

"I like mace." I turned my nose up at him.

"Well, well, you are a feisty young lady. What's your name, beautiful?" Disgust ran through my body the way he smiled and looked at me. I knew that look too well.

"We call her Jo Jo," Macey said.

Thanks, Macey. I rolled my eyes.

"Well, I sure would like to get to know you better," he winked at me. I thought, *I could squish you with one stomp*, but before I could say a word, Macey jumped in.

"Oh, Fast Jack, Robbie has eyes for her, and you know he could ruin you if he wanted to. Hands off, little man."

The short little pervert laughed and said, "Okay, okay, I'm leaving," with his hand up in the air.

We got everything unpacked and lined the chairs along the lake. "It's cocktail time," Macey said, holding up a bottle of rum.

"Let me make you a cocktail," Robbie offered. After the guy moved from his VIP spot that was the least I could do.

"Okay," I replied.

"You like sweet or strong?" he asked as he got up.

"Both," Macey chimed in.

"Let her decide," Dustin said, watching both Robbie and me.

"I guess sweet," I replied.

"And strong. I want to see Jody drunk," Macey laughed.

We all sat around in a circle in our lawn chairs, just drinking and hanging out. It was out in the open, and I kept scanning around me like I always do.

"Relax," Robbie said and grabbed my hand. "This is going to be a fun weekend." I felt relieved when Robbie grabbed my hand.

"Ok. I will try," I replied. "I must admit the rum is helping," I smiled.

"Makes it all go away." Macey held her red solo cup up to cheers.

About that time Fast Jack walked up. "Hey, party animals."

"Jack, buddy, meet Jody," Robbie said.

Jack turned every color of scared you can imagine and replied that he already had met me. I looked at Macey, and she had the biggest smirk on her face. "They already met, remember, Robbie?"

"Oh yeah, earlier today. Duh." Robbie laughed.

"Hey, Robbie, let's go over tomorrow's agenda," Jack winked and nodded to the RV. Robbie and Fast Jack disappeared into the RV.

"Do you think Fast Jack is weird?" I asked Macey and Dustin, sipping on my drink.

Macey smiled. "Absolutely, he has twisted as a pretzel, but he makes Robbie a lot of money. He wins almost every race."

"He is a puny pervert to me." I wrinkled up my nose. Macey and Dustin laughed.

Macey looked at Dustin, "Truth or dare?"

He took another sip of his beer. "You know dare, baby."

"Okay," she smiled. "I dare you to strip down and run around the track."

Thank God this was before the Internet, or Dustin would be viral. He stripped down and took off like a horse around the track, holding his privates while campers cheered him on. There were two moons out that night. One was brighter than the other.

After a few more hours went by, we decided to call it a night. Good timing, as Fast Jack came out of the RV acting shady. "Night all," he said as he rushed off.

I was a ball of nerves walking into that RV. I was thankful for the few cocktails that helped relax me. Macey and Dustin were set up in a cabin, so they could have privacy. Robbie and I were going to be alone in the RV. I made my way down the small hallway and there, sitting on the bed, was Robbie. He looked different in his eyes and was sniffling a lot. "You must be allergic to horses." I handed him a tissue.

"Something like that." He smiled and patted the bed.

"Ready for bed? No flannel tonight," he grinned.

"I will be right back." I walked into the small bathroom and stared at myself in the mirror. *Pull it together. This man likes you and it is time. No longer a little girl. Be a woman.* I slapped my face. You can do this. You have too. I walked out in a Tee shirt and shorts. "This is as sexy as it gets." I turned for him. I was thankful for that rum drink. It relaxed me and made me less nervous.

A huge grin came across Robbie's face. "Smokin' HOT." I crawled into the bed beside him, my heart racing so fast. Robbie pulled me in close to him. "I have been waiting so long to kiss you." He kissed my forehead, and I smiled. He leaned over and his lips touched my neck. Trauma Trigger.

I flashed back to the motel to the man who forced his lips on my neck as I begged him not to touch me! I pulled back. "Please don't kiss my neck, I don't like that."

"You really are a mystery, gorgeous. May I kiss your lips?" I nodded my head yes and our lips met. It wasn't a hard-forceful kiss, but it was still a trigger. My lips quivered at the thought of the last lips that touched them.

"You are so beautiful, Jody, you know that, right?"

"I guess, if you say so." I smiled.

"You know," he kissed my lips gently, "I want you." He kissed me again this time more passionately. "I want you." The words stung every part of my body. The words he spoke took me back to the worst pain I had ever felt. To the worst place I had ever been. How do I stop this feeling? How do I numb this fear? I took a death breath. I can do this. The more Robbie touched me the more I cringed. He leaned back, tracing my face with his eyes. "Do I disgust you?"

"No!" I grabbed his hand.

"The look on your face says different."

"Sorry," I mumbled. "Robbie, I like you a lot."

"You are not attracted to me?"

I felt as if I were in quicksand, sinking faster by the minute. I took another deep breath. "I am attracted to you." We started to make out more passionately. He caressed my body and it felt nice. Soft and gentle, *this I can do*. He took my hand and placed it on him. All the bright colors I felt went black.

"Nooooooo!" I screamed, jumped up and ran into the bathroom, crying and shaking. When I came back out, his eyebrows were furrowed.

He whispered, "Are you okay?"

I wiped my eyes and looked down. "No. Sorry, but I'm not ready."

"Are you a virgin?"

"Yes," I replied. I know it was a lie, but if it wasn't taken from me,

Running into Robbie

I still would have been.

"Oh, okay," he said. "I get it."

"Get what?"

"You're too young for me. I need a woman, and you're a girl." Little did he know. I was not a girl; I had been through a lot more than most women.

"It's okay," he said. "When we get back, I'll get you a bus home."

Home flashed into my mind. It was no longer safe there. The wolves would be smacking their lips waiting for me. The past would find me there. My mind raced at a million thoughts of fear a minute. "I will be right back. I need some water."

"Ok." He was less than annoyed with me. I went into the little kitchen and there on the bar sat a bottle of tequila. I took a deep breath and turned up the bottle. I was going to numb everything and do what I had to do. My body was no longer a temple that was taken from me. *My body is now a tool for survival.* My head started to get lighter by the minute. *I like this feeling,* I thought. I slipped off my shorts and crawled into that bed a sex goddess. I turned and gave Robbie the biggest kiss ever and said, "I am ready."

He looked as happy as a pervert in a porn store. I was about to give him the ride of his life that he had waited on. When he entered me, I realized quickly that Big Robbie had a little carrot. Thank God, it didn't hurt at all. *I had no idea they came in different sizes.* Afterward, I showered and got dressed, feeling very dirty again. "Don't judge me," I said in the mirror. "You know you must do what you must do to survive."

From that conversation in the mirror on, I was all over Robbie. The next day I got up and gave him the biggest hug. "Good morning," I smiled.

"Good morning to you," he smiled back.

Big Mouth Macey said, "Hmmm, what did you two do last night?"

Is it obvious? I wondered. I hiccupped behind my coffee cup. I am pretty sure I was still drunk from the night before. It worked. Tequila really does make your clothes come off.

We all headed down to the track. Macey leaned over and whispered in my ear. "Isn't sex the best thing ever?"

I shrugged my shoulders. "I guess."

"Oh, the first time is never the best," she laughed. If only she knew. I looked off in the distance to hide the tears I couldn't hold back.

The horse track was packed with people dressed in their Sunday best. I loved seeing all the big hats. One day I will wear a fancy hat, I thought to myself. We walked up to Fast Jack on the most beautiful horse. "Wow." I leaned over to Macey. "That horse has two asses." She giggled and put her hand over my mouth. The sun shone bright as the gun went off and number three was in the lead.

"GO Jack!" Robbie jumped up and down. Horse number ten came up out of nowhere, but Jack saw him out of the corner of his eye and flew across the finish line just in time. It turned out to be a fun day of winning!

I drank so much water. "Ugh, I feel horrible."

"Hair of the dog?" Macey held up the Rum.

"Oh no, none for me. I just want to go to bed."

"BED! What? Ummm, no, girl. Hair of the dog – bottoms up."

"I'll sip on a drink, but that's all."

"You and Robbie must have gotten trashed in the RV," she laughed.

"Hush, Macey." I grabbed her arm. "Robbie doesn't know I drank some tequila."

"I have created a monster," she laughed. I seriously wanted to slap her silly sometimes, but we were best friends. Or were we? Little did I know she was also a wolf in sheep's clothing, they all were…

Chapter Seven

RUNNING INTO DRUGS

After dinner, we all got our chairs and put them in a circle around the campfire as usual.

"Who wants a Jolly Rancher?" Macey asked.

"You know I do." Dustin jumped up to get it.

"I'll pass," Robbie said. Putting his hand up.

"Jody?" Macey asked, holding a piece out toward me.

"Yes, sure, I will try one."

"Here," Macey said. "Stick it under your tongue."

"Why?"

She grinned mischievously. "Less sugar gets in your teeth that way."

I accepted her answer, not knowing any better. All of those around me who I thought were my friends started laughing.

"What's so funny?" I asked.

In unison, they responded. "Nothing."

The more I sucked on the Jolly Rancher, the weirder I felt. As I sat in the middle of nowhere, things began to happen that were not normal. My body began to feel weird, and my hands and feet started to tingle. "How can my hands and feet both be asleep?" I asked.

They responded by laughing.

"I feel as though I have lockjaw, but I never had lockjaw." I pulled at my jaw. Again, they all laughed. Then everything changed around me fast! The sky became huge and the stars began to dance! It was like one of those kaleidoscopes I looked in as a kid. The colors became more vibrant! "WOW!! Do y'all see that?" I moved my head side to side trying to make out what I was seeing. I would look at Macey. "Your face looks weird. You have a big forehead racy Macey. Racy Macey. That rhymes."

They were falling over laughing at me. "Hmm." I cocked my head sideways. "All your voices are echoing." I scratched my head. "Whoa, that feels weird." I leaned over and touched Macey's face. "Your face is all squishy. You have squishy cheeks and they move around." I got super close to her face. She was laughing so hard and it echoed loudly.

I turned to Robbie, and my eyes widened. "Robbie, you have a dancing carrot with a face on your head." I tried to touch it, but it kept moving. The trees looked as if they were in 3D as they began to dance. The leaves were the most vibrant green. One tree had a little door on it. "I wonder who lives there." I walked over and started to tap on the tree with a door. Then, Winnie the Pooh opened the trunk door. "Did you see that?" I asked. It was like I was in the cartoon I used to watch as a child.

"See what?" They all laughed, falling over on top of each other.

Then there was Piglet. "Do you see Piglet, Macey?"

"I see him." She said with a giggle.

As I sat on the grass, I couldn't figure out what was going on with me. "Why is everything zooming in and out?" I asked. "Nothing will stay still." I shook my head but that only made it worse. Whooooa.

Macey laughed and said, "Girl, you're tripping."

"Tripping?" The wrinkles between my forehead wrinkled.

"Yes, I put acid on the Jolly Rancher. Just relax."

"Acid?" Oh no. "Acid that burns stuff? Is my face still there? I reached up to touch my face. "My face is squishy too." I laughed. This went on for hours. My face hurt from smiling and laughing.

They continued to ask me what I saw, and I explained in great detail how everything was so bright and vibrant! We had a fire going. Macey giggled. "Tell us about the fire, Jody."

"The fire is hot and ice, ice, baby, is cold." I broke out rapping *Ice Ice Baby* and they all laughed. "That is the biggest fire I ever saw." I reached out to touch it.

"Oh no you don't." Robbie pulled me back.

"I like you, Robbie. We did it last night."

"Yes, we did." Robbie blushed.

I talked a lot of nonsense. I went on and on about nothing, and they just laughed. The lake beside the RV was big and beautiful. I walked over to it. "What is that?" I got closer to make out what it was. "Oh WOW!" I saw Ariel from the *Little Mermaid*, my favorite movie that I watched over and over as a child. I even saw Sebastian, my favorite little crab, dancing across the water.

"WOW! This is the coolest thing ever." I started to sing *Under the Sea*. "I want to swim with them." I took off running like I ran when I was a kid, running straight for the water. Robbie chased after me and grabbed me from behind. The happy childlike thoughts went dark. My mind immediately went DARK. "Don't touch me." I kicked and screamed at him.

"Jody, calm down. It's me, Robbie."

"No, you can't take me! NO! Let me go!!" He spun me around face to face with him.

"It is me, Jody. Open your eyes." I slowly opened my eyes to see Robbie's face.

"Make it stop, please."

"I can't, baby. It has to wear off."

"Why? Why did y'all do this to me?" Robbie took me back to where Macey and Dustin were. Their faces turned from laughing hyenas into wolves. What is going on? I was so scared. My heart raced. *I can't trust these people in front of me. They are wolves too.* "I have to go to the rest room," and I ran into the Macey's cabin.

One thing you never want to do when taking acid is look in a mirror. When I flipped on the light and looked at myself, my face was so damaged. My nose was on my forehead. It looked like someone cut off all the parts of my face and glued them back in the wrong place. I started to cry. *Oh, no, I destroyed my face with acid.*

I had to get out of there, but I still had to pee. I sat down on the toilet, and my trip went bad fast. I hate spiders more than just about anything. This huge web spun around me. It sends shivers down my spine to remember it. It was the biggest spiderweb I have ever seen. Then the big black spider came to get me. He was huge with the long furry legs, and he stood tall as the ceiling as he was coming to get me. He inched in closer and closer. I jumped up off the toilet and the spider crawled toward me.

"Let me out!" I cried. The spider started toward me again and its face turned to the man who raped me. I began to scream at the top of my lungs. "Help!"

Robbie and Macey came running in. "OMG, what's wrong?" Macey tried to comfort me.

I pushed her off! "You did this to me!" My face was red with anger. I turned to Robbie. "Kill it!" I screamed, fear running through my body.

"Kill what?" they both confusingly looked around.

"Kill the BIG black spider!" I insisted.

"Oh no," I heard Macey whisper to Robbie. "Her hit went bad."

"What the heck does that even mean?!" I screamed. "I want my Mom now! I'm going to call her."

I ran across the room, and Robbie put his hand on the phone. "You can't, Jody. It's three o'clock in the morning."

"Let me go!" I picked up the phone, hands trembling, trying to dial the number as snot rolled down my face.

"No, baby. Sorry you can't." Robbie hung up the phone and unplugged it from the wall. I couldn't breathe. My breaths were coming faster and faster, but I couldn't control them.

"I can't breathe." I screamed.

"What do we do?" Macey was rushing around the room. "Jody, what can we do to help you?"

Then, in my mind, I remembered a scripture that got me through my worst night. "Yea, though I walk through the valley of the shadow of death, I will fear no evil. For thou art with me; thy rod and thy staff they comfort me."

"Find me a Bible now!" I screamed. The big black spider was coming closer and closer. Robbie found a Bible in the drawer and handed it to me. I quickly repeated, "I will fear no evil. I will fear no evil. I will fear no evil," and the web and big black spider slowly disappeared. My muscles started to relax, and I could breathe again.

When I woke up, the Bible was still lying on my chest. I quickly looked around to see if anything moved. I had begged the night before for Robbie to tell me how I know the "trip" is over. "Everything goes back to normal." He kissed my forehead.

I looked around the room and everything was back to normal. I looked beside me and saw Robbie sleeping next to me. *That was sweet of him,* I thought. I woke him up, and he wanted some loving. "Sorry, buddy, I have the biggest headache because you drugged me last night."

He grinned. "Not me. Macey did."

As we walked into the RV, Macey and Dustin were eating breakfast. "You took over our cabin and we took over the RV." Macey was making me some coffee.

"Good morning," smiled Macey, her eyes wide.

"Is it?" I asked her. "Is this 'special coffee' too?" I rolled my eyes, hurt by my friend.

"Jody, I am sorry. I thought it would be fun. I never thought you would have a bad hit. Let's leave the past in the past. It's a new day," she stated with her usual optimism. I sipped my coffee, silent and furious.

As we stood by the track later on, Macey leaned over and whispered in my ear. "Are you still mad at me?"

"Not mad," I replied, not taking my eyes off of the track. "Disappointed."

"Sorry, girl. I just thought you needed to loosen up."

"That's probably true," I replied, "but please tell me before you drug me."

"Okay," she laughed. "I promise."

Fast Jack finished second that day and came running up to

Robbie. "Hey, Robbie, you up for the white horse tonight?"

"I am in," replied Robbie.

What's the white horse? I wondered. I saw brown horses, but no white horses. *I bet the white horse is gorgeous.* I thought to myself.

"We're getting low on beer," Dustin said as we walked back to the RV.

"We'll go grab some," Macey replied.

We rode in silence for miles. "Jody. I just can't take the silence. Please forgive me."

I stared out the window. "I am trying," I said, still looking away from her.

Macey grabbed my hand. "Jody. I am so sorry, from the very bottom of my heart."

I turned to her with tears in my eyes. "That really scared me last night."

"I know. Me too, Jody. I have never seen a trip go bad. I just thought it would be fun."

I looked out the window thinking, you have no clue what I have been through. I grabbed Macey's hand with my other hand. "I forgive you."

Macey smiled. "Thank you."

We finally got to the store that was almost an hour away. I hated being out in the middle of nowhere with no protection. "Are you going in?"

"I will stay in the car."

"Okay." Macey jumped out and I immediately locked the doors. I felt like such coward, but the fear in me would not let me move my legs. Once again, I was frozen to that spot.

Running into Drugs

When we got back to the RV I said, "Wonder where everyone went?"

Macey laughed. "I bet they are stuffing their faces."

I grabbed the bags and walked inside. There were Robbie, Dustin and Fast Jack around the kitchen table, and it had lines of white powder on it. My mouth and the bags dropped. Robbie was bent over the lines, snorting one of them with a rolled-up hundred-dollar bill. All their backs were to me so they didn't know I saw them. I slowly closed the RV door and took off running.

I had only seen cocaine in the movies. When I was little my cousins and I would sneak and watch R-rated movies. One time, Mawmaw caught us watching one on cable TV, and we got a good spanking. Now here I am in a horror movie once again. Macey was getting the last of the bags out of the car. I ran past her.

"What's wrong?" she yelled after me.

"Leave me alone!" I yelled back. I found a barn where all the race horses were and bent down. With my knees pulled into my chest, I cried like a baby. What have I gotten myself into? Who are these people? I didn't feel safe at all.

Now here I am in a barn by myself with no one once again to protect me. My heart started to race, and the anxiety took over. I turned and threw up beside me. What if an unknown man finds me, rapes me? I'm all alone. What if I get kidnapped? None of my family know I am here. I would just disappear without a trace. The "man" I trusted has illegal drugs on the table in our RV. Now I have to worry about drugs, too! I am surrounded by people I can't trust.

As I cried, I heard footsteps. With fear rushing through me, I scrambled to hide deeper inside the stall. My body trembled as I held my breath.

"Jody, I hear you," Macey said. "It's okay." I exhaled a breath of relief.

I whispered, "I'm down here."

"Girl, what the heck is wrong with you? You're shaking so hard. Jody, OMG did you throw up?" Macey wrapped her arms around me to slow my breathing down. "Jody, please tell me what is it?" she whispered.

"Cocaine," I whispered back.

Macey gave me the calmest smile. "Jody, calm down. I know you're new to all this. I am sorry it upset you."

"I don't belong here, Macey. I don't belong anywhere."

"Jody, why would you say that?"

"I don't do drugs. I barely got used to tequila and now cocaine." The tears fell harder down my face. "I just…I just can't believe my life."

Macey lifted my head. "You don't have to do it too."

I looked at her, confusion in my eyes. "I don't?"

"No, silly," she said. "Come on, girl, let's go back inside." She got up and held her hand out to help me up too.

As we walked in, Robbie, Dustin and Fast Jack all scrambled to "hide" the evidence on the table. "You can remove the dish towel, guys. Jody already saw it." Macey walked over and picked up the dish towel to reveal the plastic bag filled with powder.

Robbie walked over to me and put his arm around my shoulder. "You okay, beautiful?"

I stood there numb to my feelings, overwhelmed once again. "I'm okay." I nodded my head.

Dustin walked over to Macey and smacked her on the butt. "You want a bump, baby doll?"

Macey looked at me and then the table. She mouthed "sorry" to me and turned to Dustin. "You know I do, handsome."

And there went the only friend I had as she started to do a line, too. You know how in the woods, wolves surround their prey. They don't attack right away; they circle first. I could feel the pressure of the wolves circling. I knew if I wasn't a wolf they would take me out of the pack. They wouldn't want "miss goody two shoes" around anymore. I took a deep breath. I knew what I had to do. I could no longer be a scared little sheep, it was time to join the wolves.

"Can I try?" I whispered. You would have thought it was Christmas the way they all lit up.

"That's my girl," replied Macey, handing me the rolled-up bill. My stomach turned at the thought of the person I was. I leaned over and snorted the devil's dynamite. OUCH! It burned as it went up my nose, and the taste in my mouth was dreadful.

I instantly had a huge wave rush through my body - a mix of excitement and fire. Thank God that nothing moved like acid tripping. This was a totally different feel, and I didn't hate it. My eyes, however, never closed to sleep for two days. It was like an energy drink times ten. I just wanted to go and go and go. My teeth were numb and that felt weird. The best part was it numbed me emotionally. I didn't have a care in the world. It turned me into a sex goddess!

"Baby, not again." Robbie lay back exhausted.

"Again," I teased him. I wasn't afraid of sex at all on cocaine. It took every emotion away.

It sickens me to think of how much money went up my nose. My dad worked so hard for his money and here was his baby girl snorting all this money up her nose. The more the guilt came, the more cocaine I wanted to do. I didn't care. Those three days went by so fast. *That is why they call it the "white horse,"* I thought. I sat on the couch in the RV looking all around me. Feels like another nightmare, but this is my life. Fast Jack was hyped up more than any of us. I thought the guy was going to have a heart attack. I now understood where he got his name.

By the next morning we had finally sobered up. The high was fun, but the low was very low. I instantly thought of my family whom I hadn't called in over two weeks. I made a decision that as soon as we got home, I would call my mom if it wasn't too late at night.

The phone rang. My dad answered. "Hi, Daddy."

"Hold on I will get your momma." He wouldn't talk to me, he wouldn't acknowledge me. I can't say I blamed him.

My mom answered the phone. "Hey, baby, how are you?"

"I am good," I lied.

"How are your new friends?" she asked.

Oh, ya know, they have me doing cocaine, I thought. Instead, I said, "Good, Mom. They really care about me. We just went to the horse races."

"Oh, wow!"

"Yes. It was so much fun, Mom." I painted the perfect picture of my perfect life.

"Well everyone misses you terribly, baby."

"Everyone but Daddy," I whispered.

"You know your daddy is upset, but he misses you too. Please come home soon, baby."

Tears swelled up in my eyes. "I can't, Mom."

"I love you."

"I love you too."

When we got back we went upstairs to unpack. I walked in the bathroom, and my mouth flew open. "Robbie!" His nose was pouring blood, and he was trying to get it to stop. "Robbie, did cocaine do that?"

"Yeah," he replied. "It's the nasal tissue."

"Has it happened before?" I walked over closer to him.

"Yeah, baby, it has."

I sat him down and said, eyeball to eyeball, "No more, please. I care about you."

He looked at me and smiled. "Okay, baby, no more."

*****

He kept his word, or did he? We had been at this house for probably six months. We loved living there. Robbie and I were in the "I love you" phase and he made me happy.

Life was kind of back to normal. My anxiety seemed to be better and I felt safe living there. So safe that I walked the neighborhood alone. That was a big deal for me. One day I was running late and had to walk at dusk on my usual lap around the neighborhood. The homes around me were massive and all landscaped to the max. I could see golfers way off in the distance. I would wave at some; others I would act as if I didn't see them.

I couldn't help but notice a car behind me. At first, I thought the driver lived there and would pass by me. Cars would pass me all the time. I walked slower, but the car never passed me. I darted across one of the yards, and the car turned. Oh good, I breathed a sigh of relief. When I turned onto the next road my blood ran cold as headlights flashed on from a car parked on the side of the road facing me. OMG it was the same car!

Fear shot through me, and I knew that I was being chased. *It is THEM!* shot through my head like a bullet to a target. *No. Please God, no! They found me!* I immediately cut through the yards beside me, running so fast my heart almost beat out of my chest.

No way I was going back to my house, so instead I went to the house right beside me. I knocked on the door, but there wasn't an answer, so I began to beat on the door. *Please, God, please someone open the door. Help. Please open the door!*

An older man opened the door and I pushed past him. "I am sorry, but someone is chasing me."

"Who?"

"A car." I couldn't talk for crying. I was in a complete panic attack. "I can't breathe," I said.

"I'm a doctor," the man said. "Hang on." He went to the kitchen and brought out a paper bag. "Breathe in this," he said. "What are you running from?"

Everything, I thought. But I said, "A man was chasing me in a car."

"How do you know he was chasing you, sweetie?"

"Everywhere I went, he went." I breathed into the bag some more. "He…" The words wouldn't form. I started to breathe into the paper bag. My whole body shook. I was so scared.

"It's okay." The man tried to comfort me by patting me on the back. "Call the police, honey," he told his wife.

I kept trying to call Robbie, but he was at a work dinner and not answering. Every time he didn't answer I got angrier. The police arrived and asked me a bunch of questions. I could only tell them limited details about the man because he was in the car and the windows were tinted. I only saw him through the front windshield. The police combed the area looking for the car I described to him, but they walked back into the house with no results.

The phone rang and we all jumped. "Your wife is here, and she is pretty shaking up," the lady spoke into the phone.

Wife? "Girlfriend," I corrected her. She just shook her head like, whatever dear, and handed me the phone. "Here, sweetie, he wants to talk to you."

"Hello? Jody what in the world is going on? I am in the middle of a very important meeting."

"A car was following me, and I was scared."

"Give me fifteen minutes; I am on my way."

I sat on this nice couple's couch, my breathing finally returning to normal. "Would you like some tea?" The lady came in with the cutest tea pot.

"Thank you," I smiled. The couple looked to be in their late 80s but she had the prettiest skin and silver hair that bounced as she walked. She sat down beside me. We all jumped as someone knocked on the door.

It was Robbie and his face looked as red as his hair. He walked over and took my hand. "She's okay. Thank you for taking care of her." As we got outside I told Robbie I really needed a hug. "I think you are being a little overdramatic, Jody."

"Overdramatic?" I turned to him and noticed the scent coming off his collar.

"Do you smell like perfume?" Heat flushed through my body. Was this the important meeting he had? I leaned in close and took a better sniff. "You do smell like perfume and that isn't my scent."

"Jody, calm down. The woman I met with hugged me goodbye; that is all."

"She hugged you 'bye?'" Steam started oozing out of my ears. It was then I realized that his dinner meeting was much more than dinner. I was so angry as I flew up the stairs. "You jerk!" I screamed at him. "Who is she?"

"No one," he replied, rubbing his hands through his red hair.

"Liar!" I screamed. I knew he was lying. "You make me sick."

"I do? Well then maybe it is time for you to go home," Robbie snapped at me while taking off his tie. "I did nothing wrong but have a dinner meeting. If you can't trust me, Jody, you can leave! This is my house, not yours. I will get you a way home," and he slammed the bedroom door.

I held my stomach. *I can't go home. I have no choice.* I walked into the living room where Robbie was drinking a beer and watching TV. I crawled up in his lap. "Sorry, I was overdramatic," I smiled.

Nose to nose he spoke the words that ripped out my heart. "I think you are too young for me. I think you need to go home." My mind raced to home. *I can't go back.*

I started to kiss Robbie hard and passionately. He couldn't resist me. "Are we alone?" I whispered.

"Yes. Dustin and Macey are at the movies."

"Lucky you," I replied. I am not proud of what I did next, but let's just say it changed his mind when I was done.

The next morning Robbie woke me up early with coffee. "I had something to tell you last night but got sidetracked."

"After coffee," I smiled. After coffee he shut the bedroom door. I got dressed and went into Robbie's office. "Okay, I am all ears. Baby, what's the big news?"

"You might want to sit down." Robbie got up and sat beside me and took my hand.

"Sweetheart. What? Robbie, you're making me nervous. What?"

"I have good news and bad news."

"What's the good news?"

He leaned over, grabbing my hand. "I paid off my debt, so we are safe."

My head thought it was going to fly off my shoulders. *What the heck is going on?* "I hate to ask," I cringed at the words, "but what is the bad news?"

"Jody, we must move again. We need to be out in two weeks."

Move Again? I thought. My mind raced. "Where are we going now?"

Chapter Eight

FEAR AND PAYBACKS

Those two weeks flew by. Packing and boxes were my life. I was starting to get used to it. We didn't move out of the area, just from the big, beautiful house. Robbie was broke. He used all the money he had to pay off his drug debt. He still had his RV, though, and that made him happy. "Are we going to live in it?" I asked over dinner.

"No, silly. I have another house we are renting." With curiosity I wondered where that was.

When we left the big, beautiful home on the golf course, I must admit I was a little relieved. I don't think I could ever feel safe in that neighborhood again. I knew the man in that car was after me. He wasn't connected to my past, but Robbie owed him a lot of money. I was still the target. Thank God, the old couple took me in. I had to shake off the thoughts of "what if."

As we pulled up to our new house my heart sank. It was a big house, but it was older, with black bars on the windows. The paint had peeled off, it and the structure didn't look secure. The area looked rough. "Well this is home," Robbie smiled.

I tried to be supportive, but fear covered me. No way was I walking in this neighborhood. "We will make the best of it, baby," I smiled.

The mood from everyone was somber. Weeds had won against the grass and were everywhere. Some of the windows were broken out and the porch looked like it could cave in at any moment. Robbie wiped the cobwebs off the front door. A shiver went down my spine. He opened the door, and it smelled of stale cigarette smoke and mildew.

Macey leaned over and whispered in my ear. "Nothing a little TLC can't fix." I had to smile; the girl was optimistic. Macey and Dustin took the upstairs room, and Robbie and I had the master bedroom on the bottom floor. It was a change for sure from the three-story house we were in before. Dead bugs were everywhere. *Even the bugs couldn't survive here.* I thought

"The rental company had it sprayed." Robbie grabbed a broom and swept up the dead bugs.

"Thank God." I replied.

"You'll like it." Robbie looked up at me.

"It will grow on me, I hope." I don't know what it was about this house, but the moment I walked in, fear ran through me. I had the worst eerie feeling. I had to shake it off because beggars can't be choosers. I'm sure it was mostly because of the area. It was rundown and reminded me a lot of the area close to the motel.

"I make money fast, sweetheart." Robbie poked out his chest. "We will have this place a masterpiece in no time."

"Yeah, we will." Macey reached up and gave Robbie a high five.

With a fresh coat of paint in each room, new floors and some TLC it was starting to feel like home. The only thing I hated was the neighborhood our house was in. This neighborhood was a big trigger for me. Bars on windows and graffiti everywhere screamed danger to me. Robbie started working away from home a lot with Macey and Dustin. I hated being in this house all day long by myself. The emptiness was so quiet, and I jumped at every little noise I heard. I felt like a prisoner locked in a house of fear.

Robbie and the gang came home after work one day and I made them dinner as usual. As I was putting the food on the table, I told them I had a very important announcement.

"You're Prego!" Macey jumped up to hug me while Robbie spit his beer across the table.

"Umm, no." I put my hand up to stop Macey. "I am getting a job." They all turned to each other in confusion.

"How, sweetie?" Robbie asked.

"Well," I replied, "I saw in the paper where this temp agency is looking for a receptionist and I am good at that. The lady on the phone already said she had something in mind for me."

Robbie leaned back in his chair. "I don't know, baby. You don't have a car."

I slammed the ketchup on the table. "That is because I don't have a flipping job!"

Macey giggled. "Makes sense, Robbie."

"Hush, Macey." Robbie turned to me. "Is this what you really want?"

"It is." My eyes begged for him to say yes.

"Okay." I hugged him so tight I thought his head was going to pop off.

"Easy, baby." He peeled me off.

"Thank you so much, Robbie." My insides were so happy. I wasn't going to have to be alone in the house all day anymore.

Fear and Paybacks

The following Monday I was very nervous as Robbie dropped me off. "You will do great, baby." He kissed me on the forehead. "Have a good day."

"Thank you."

I walked into this huge, intimidating building. I could hear the devil in my ear: *No one wants a high school dropout like you.* I pushed it to the back of my mind. I have to land this job permanently. I walked in and was greeted by Dawn.

"Hi, can we help you?" I thought I had a country accent, but this girl took the cake.

"I'm here as a temp for the front desk job."

"Oh," said Dawn. "You need Nicki."

She disappeared to find her, and I stood in this big building with people rushing all around me. A few minutes later, Nicki appeared. She was dressed nicely and professionally. I could tell she was a power woman in charge of this place. She smiled sweetly at me and held out her hand to shake mine. "Come with me."

I followed her into her huge office. I was as nervous as one person could ever be talking to her. I just knew she was going to see straight through me. As she began to talk, I noticed she had a bit of a stutter. That was music to my ears. *Look at her - a power house running this whole company - not letting some little stutter stop her!*

I was so excited. I believe at that moment, she and I connected. Nicki set me up, and everything she said, every time she spoke, I listened. I wanted to learn as much as I could from this woman.

When I got back to our house, I was so excited to tell Robbie all of my good news. He was too busy in Robbie world to care. "Listen, baby, I need to talk to you," he said. "The reason we had to move to this rough area is because I lost a good amount of money gambling."

"And drugs," I replied.

He jerked his head back in shock. "I quit that."

"Did you?" I asked.

He then stormed off into the other room. When he came back, he promised me that this really was the end of cocaine. I stood firm, arms crossed in front of me. "One more time, and I will leave."

"I know baby, I know." He gave a half-smile.

It is crazy how you can have such a great day at work and come home to a depressing place. We had been at the new house a couple of months. It wasn't horrible anymore. We all had adjusted to it well, although I still hated our bedroom being on the bottom floor.

Nights and weekends everyone was home – my favorite time. We would cook out or just watch TV together and veg out. A few weeks after I started working Macey came in my room. "I have some news." She plopped down on the bed.

"What is that?" I started to remove my makeup.

"I am going home to Texas to visit!" She was grinning from ear to ear with excitement. "My mom and dad said you can come too."

"That's so exciting!" We were now jumping up and down with excitement like toddlers jumping on the bed.

"When, Macey?"

"For a whole week!" I felt like a balloon and all my air just seeped out.

"A week?" My smile was now upside down.

"Yes." Macey nodded her head. "What is the problem?"

"My job."

"Just quit," she laughed.

Fear and Paybacks

"Macey, I can't just quit. I really like it there and I want them to hire me full time."

"Well then, you don't get to see Texas." Macey tipped her imaginary hat and walked out of the room. Part of me wanted to chase after her. *You are right, forget that job. I can find a new one. I mean, it is Atlanta. There are tons of jobs,* but the other part of me, the part with the heart, couldn't do that to Nicki. She was so kind to me. She didn't judge me, and a small part of me felt she believed in me. The way she looked at me gave me hope.

I walked into the living room where Macey and Dustin were in the recliner arguing. "I will miss you more."

"No, baby, I will miss you more." He kissed her playfully.

"It's a tie," I interrupted and sat down on the couch.

"You won't miss me more; you're going to the race track," Macey giggled. My world stopped spinning.

"What?"

"Big mouth." Dustin covered Macey's mouth.

"What are you talking about, Macey?" Robbie walked in. I jumped up and gave him a hug.

"So, I heard we are going back to the races?" Robbie shot a look to Macey and Dustin.

"Not me." Dustin held up his hands.

Robbie grabbed my hand and led me over to the couch. "Sit down, sweetie. Macey, Dustin, can you give us space?"

"Sure thing." Dustin jumped up, knocking Macey onto the floor. "Sorry, doll." He picked her up, throwing her over his shoulder. "We are off to bed."

Robbie faced me. "Baby, I have to go to the races and win some money." Robbie loved to gamble on anything from horses to speed boats.

"Robbie, you just got into all that trouble and now you're gambling again?"

"Baby, I need to you to understand that I can make a lot of money."

I looked down at the floor, a million thoughts a minute running through my mind. I was in no place to argue. "Okay, sweetie, when do we leave?"

Robbie took a deep breath as he shifted from side to side. "Baby, you can't go." The words came out like slow motion.

"WHAT!" I jumped back in horror. "Why not? Since when?"

"Jody, it's an all-boys trip."

The tears started falling down my face. "Please," I begged. "Please don't leave me in this big house alone ALL NIGHT."

Robbie held me tight. "It's okay, baby."

"No, it's not. You can't leave me here alone."

"I must go, sweetheart. I must make back the money I lost. Jody, nothing you can say or do is going to change my mind. I will be back before you know it."

"When do you leave?"

"Tomorrow morning, after we drop off Macey at the airport."

"Okay." I lowered my head and walked out of the room.

The sound of the RV pulling out the next day sounded like a million demons celebrating. The fear in my body was paralyzing me. As it got later in the day anxiety overtook me. If I had had something to numb me, I would have taken a lot of it.

I hated this time in my life. I would never walk by windows, only crawl under them so no one would see me. I checked every window and every door to make sure they were locked. I put booby traps under the windows so if someone broke in I would hear it. I went into the kitchen and got enough food and alcohol to last me three days. I was going to stay drunk the whole time they were gone. I also grabbed the biggest knife out of the kitchen. If someone was coming for me, I wasn't going down without a bloody fight. To make sure no one got in my bedroom I pushed our huge dresser drawer in front of the door. I got in the closet and sat on the floor, knife beside me.

I called my sister who was always there for me. "Melissa?"

"Yes, Jody? Where the heck are you? You have Mom and Dad worried sick!"

"I rode the white horse, and now I am going to die." I pulled my knees close to my chest. "They are coming to get me. I am not safe. Any minute, Melissa, I will disappear."

"You rode the what?"

"Drugs, sis. I did drugs, I saw Winnie the Pooh, his house, Piglet, Arial, and a huge black spider. Then I did cocaine. It burned up my nose and now I feel I am going to die in this house."

"Are you on drugs now? Jody, you have to calm down. I can't understand a word you are saying."

"No. I am drinking, but no drugs." I hung my head between my knees, crying so hard snot ran all down my face.

"Jody, I am coming to get you!"

"No, Melissa, you can't." I was starting to slur my words. "The big black wolf will get me."

"Jody, what in the world are you talking about?"

"Melissa, I am so scared." I was trembling.

"Jody, let me come get you and bring you home."

Home, I thought. *If only I could.*

"I can't, sissy. I love you. I have to go."

"Jody, I love you too. I am worried about you."

"I am worried about me too, sissy." I hung up the phone and lay on the floor and cried.

This was like the ultimate scary movie, but I couldn't escape it. The devils started in with horrible thoughts. *You are all alone. Just think of the people who saw them leave.* At night the neighbors were loud. I would hear glass break or horns honking, people yelling, and even gunshots. It was terrifying. I would drink more. *This house isn't safe.* I would drink even more. I needed to numb me. I couldn't deal with real life. I couldn't deal with being alone with my thoughts.

The days crept by. There was no way for me to call Robbie, so I sat in that closet and drank. I drank until I threw up and then I drank some more. Fear was all around me in that closet. Chains were not physically on me, but mentally I was bound by them.

I didn't leave that closet for three days. I used the bathroom, but that was it. I didn't eat or sleep, I barely ate, and I drank a lot. I woke up when I heard the RV pull up but wondered if it was Robbie or someone else in our yard.

I slowly tiptoed down the hall and peeked out of the window. Yes, it was him. I was so excited, I ran to my bathroom to make myself not look like one of the walking dead. Three nights without sleep will do that. I put the knife back in the kitchen and hid all the empty bottles. I was so excited my sweetheart was home.

I ran into the living room to give Robbie the biggest hug and stopped suddenly when I saw two women in my living room. One was a short brunette and the other was a tall skinny blonde. The brunette was in short shorts and a halter top, and the blonde had on a mini skirt and a skin-tight tank top that her fake boobs didn't fit. My blood pressure went sky high! I was PISSED!

I asked, "Um, why are you in my living room?"

The brunette said, "Oh, because they're unloading the RV." My anger was at an all-time high. I thought of the knife in the kitchen. *I will cut you.* I shook off the thought.

"And who are you?" I asked.

"Jessica," the brunette replied. "I am Fast Jack's girlfriend, and this is my friend Katie."

"Nice to meet you," Katie said with a big grin, her hand reaching for mine. I reached out and shook her hand. I'm surprised it didn't burn her, as mad as I was.

"Let me ask you something," I said. "Did you both go on the trip?" I couldn't keep calm. I paced back and forth like a tiger ready to attack. Steam was probably coming out of both my ears at this point. "Sorry, I am confused." "I was told girlfriends weren't going on this trip."

"Oh," Katie said. "Maybe we should go." She grabbed Katie's hand.

"Not so fast." I stepped in front of her. I was shaking, I was so mad. "So why is it that you girls got to go and I didn't?"

The blonde spoke up "That is probably because we went to a strip club. Some girlfriends don't like that." My eyes popped out of my head. By this point, I could have pulled every single strand of this girl's hair out of her head and strangled her with it. "We really need to go." Jessica tried to walk past me again.

About that time, Fast Jack came in the room. He said a few curse words. "Hey, Fast Jack," I spat at him.

"Ladies, we said go straight to the truck. What are you doing in here?"

"We had to pee," Jessica giggled.

About that time, Robbie walked in. The look on his face was priceless.

"Busted," I said with a smirk. "Everyone GET OUT!" I pointed to the front door. They all ran out. I slammed and locked the front door. I walked right past Robbie and stormed off into the bedroom and slammed the door. I was so pissed. I took out my suitcase and began to pack.

He walked behind me, trying to hug me. I pushed him off. "Don't touch me!"

"I hate you!" I pulled clothes out of my dresser and threw them in my suitcase.

"Baby, listen," he said. "I didn't know they were all going."

"Whatever," I screamed. "You have no idea the hell I have been going through here alone. I was so scared, and you are off in strip clubs partying it up with Jessica and Katie. You told me NO girls were going. I am so pissed at you. You disgust me."

"Please don't leave. Where would you go?" he pleaded with a whisper.

The words, like dynamite, hit me so hard. I knew I had to forgive him because I had nowhere else to go. I began to cry, and he came over and put his arms around me. "I love you. Please don't leave." He kissed me on top of my head.

"I know you cheated on me with that blonde bimbo." I tried to hold back the tears.

"No, sweetheart, I would never do that."

I knew he was lying, but once again what choice did I have? I knew I had to forgive him, so he wouldn't forget about me. "If you ever cheat on me again, I will be gone. I will live on the streets if I have to." I was so upset at him and wanted to pay him back so badly; instead, I ended up in the bed with him. I used my body as a tool to survive again.

"Man, I sure am hungry." He rubbed his big bare belly.

I leaned over and gave him a kiss. "I can go get Whataburger for you."

"Oh, baby, that sounds so good."

"Yes, it does to me too." My mind wasn't on food; my mind was on payback.

I slipped on my shoes. "I'm taking your truck."

Anger was flooding through my body. That jerk! What could I do to pay him back? I thought about laxatives in his burger, but that might be obvious. *Think, Jody, think.*

I smiled an evil smile to myself. I knew exactly what I was going to do. Robbie drove this big, old Southern Comfort truck, the kind that flares out on the sides. It was green and mean and his baby.

"Never, ever take it through the drive thru," he had told me over and over.

"Why not?" I asked.

"Baby, a drive-thru will rip the paint right off it. A truck like mine can't fit through a drive-thru. Promise me you will never go through a drive-thru."

"Okay, baby, I won't," I always replied. *Until you leave me at home ALONE and run off with other women and go to strip clubs and screw them.* My blood pressure was at an all-time high. Fury filled every vein in my body.

I pulled into the restaurant driveway, the truck barely fitting.

I turned the wheel with a screech. It sounded like fingernails on a chalkboard, but it was music to my ears. I hit the gas some more, and the sound got louder. I got up to the drive-thru window and opened the door. "Oh, damn."

The drive-thru employee looked out the window. "I don't think that truck fits through here, ma'am." I could tell he was trying to keep from laughing his butt off. I glanced out of the window at my beautiful artwork.

"Yeah, that might need some bodywork." I smiled. "Do you have a few raw onions I can get on the side?"

"Sure," the guy smiled strangely at me. I enjoyed my French fries on the way home, looking in the rearview mirror at the orange paint running all along the side of his truck.

I got home and a little raw onion turned on the water works. "Robbie," I screamed.

He came running, "What's wrong, baby?"

"I think I scratched your truck in the drive-thru."

"What!" He jumped up. "I told you to never take it through the drive-thru!"

He flew out the door, and I could hear him cussing up a storm. He came back in and slammed the door. "Wow, Jody, seriously my truck is jacked up. That is over a thousand dollars in damage."

"I know," I whispered. "Sorry, babe. I had no idea how close I was." I was hugging him so he couldn't see the evil smile I had. I say evil because I know it was evil. I wanted to hurt him like he hurt me.

The next day Macey came home. I was so excited to have girl time while Robbie and Dustin were gone to work. "How was your weekend?" she asked.

"Horrible," I replied. "I hid myself in the closet for three days."

"Why?" Macey looked concerned.

"Robbie and the boys left me here alone while they went out with girls and strippers."

Macey was a redhead, and if you think I could get mad, it was nothing like when Macey did. She turned to me, red in the face. "Did you say girls and strippers?"

"I did," I replied proudly.

Her eyes narrowed. "What girls? Dustin told me it was going to be all guys." This woman looked like a snake ready to strike.

"Well, Dustin is a liar because two of them were in our living room." Macey turned and punched the wall as hard as she could.

"I am pissed," Macey, jutting her chin out.

"I know," I nodded in agreement.

"No, I am pissed!" she screamed. I had never seen this side of Macey. She was like a cat when all its hair stands up. I knew I needed to calm her down before she took off looking for a gun.

"I can make you laugh," I said.

"How?"

"I tore up the side of Robbie's truck."

Surprisingly, she didn't laugh. "I am glad you got your revenge. But Jody, that's not good enough. I am so pissed." She started to pace back and forth, still holding the same pillow she was taking her anger out on. I felt sorry for the pillow.

"Macey, I am pissed too. You have no idea. The last three days were pure torture for me. I called in to work today, and I hated to do that, but I am mentally and physically exhausted."

"We need to pay these jerks back. We need the ultimate payback."

"What you got in mind?" I winked at her, intrigued by her mindset.

"I got it." Macey had the evilest smile I had ever seen.

"We all know how much Robbie loves his big RV. The one they just did God knows what in." I rolled my eyes. "Yes, I have a plan."

"I'm listening," I said, getting excited about what was to come.

"We know how much Dustin loves the stereo system in it," she continued. I could almost see the wheels turning in her head.

"Yes, but what does that have to do with anything?" I asked.

"Be right back," Macey said before running to her room. When she came back, she held two baseball bats. "One for you, and one for me," she smiled.

My eyes opened wide. "Oh no, we can't," I replied.

She looked me dead in my eyes. "Jody. This man left you at home ALONE while he partied it up with Katie." She got right up in my face. "You know Katie was all over your man."

I could feel the fire in my belly growing.

She glared harder. "You know he spent all that money on strippers, and they were all over his body too, touching him while he touched all over them and Katie watched on the sidelines waiting for her turn. She had sex with him in your bed."

I got sicker and sicker with every word she said. Then she said the final straw. "You know he left you here all alone scared in a closet while he did it."

That was it. That was the trigger. Fire flew from every part of my body. I turned to her and with an evil grin and said, "I am in!" My adrenaline was pumping as I busted out the windows on the RV. "This feels so good." I smiled at Macey. "This is for leaving me when

I begged you not to go." I swung and hit the RV hard as glass went flying.

"You are right; this is the perfect payback, Macey."

Macey turned to me "Now for the good part."

"Good part? I thought this was the good part." Heck this was the great part!

"Oh no," she said. "Start stealing, girl."

"Steal? I don't understand Macey. What do you mean?"

"Well, to be honest, it isn't *stealing*."

"It's not?" I asked. I was so confused at where this was going. "We have to hurry before they get back."

"We love them, and they stole our time and our hearts." She sure knew how to push my buttons.

"Yeah, they did," I replied.

"Well it's time we returned the favor," she smiled, and jerked Dustin's brand-new stereo out of the console.

"OMG, Macey."

"Grab the microwave, let's put in all in my car." I couldn't believe I was doing this. Macey handed me items and I placed them in her trunk. Before I knew it, we had cleaned that RV out. "Good job." Macey smiled at me. "Now let's go to the pawn shop," and we did high fives with the baseball bats. We got back to the house and poured some wine. Onions? Got it. Tissues? Got it. We had our evil plan, and the devil danced with delight.

Macey looked at me and said, "Ready?"

I nodded and called Robbie. I knew how to turn it on as an actress if I needed to, and I did right then.

"Hello?"

"OMG, baby." I was crying into the phone. "Macey and I just got home, and your RV got broken into. Robbie, they took everything."

"What?!" he screamed.

"Yes, I am so scared and shaking. Please come home."

"Okay. Okay. Dustin and I are on the way."

I hung up the phone and gave Macey a smile. When Robbie and Dustin got there, they ran straight to the RV. Panic was all over their faces. They called the police, but the only fingerprints that came up belonged to Robbie, Dustin, Macey, me, and random ones from their party weekend.

"Next time, don't have so many people in your RV," I said and walked inside the house sipping my wine. They never did find out it was Macey and me. Until now…

*****

Work was going great. I had been there almost two months, and I had been promoted from being a temp to a full-time position, thanks to Nicki and Tee. I talked to Nicki some about Robbie, and she kept telling me I deserved better.

I liked that I could talk to her. Nicki was like a mom boss to me. I could tell she cared. I also loved Tee, the receptionist. The company had just been bought and Tee was getting promoted from receptionist to accounting, so I took her place.

When she looked at me, it was like she could look through me. We became great friends and spent a lot of time together, so I told her some of what was going on with Robbie. I loved to go to work because it was an escape for me. Plus, I liked making my own money, even if it was only a little bit. Tee told me anytime I was scared I could come to her house. That made me feel so good. I told her, "You don't know how much that means to me."

Fear and Paybacks

"I think I do," she smiled at me.

One day, I came home from work, and Robbie had a suitcase packed sitting at the door. I stared at it for a moment. "Going somewhere?" I asked.

"Yeah," he replied. "Fast Jack needs some help working on his boat, so I'm going over there to help him."

"You are going to Kentucky?" I put my hands on my hips.

"No, silly. Jack lives in Alabama about two hours away tops!" Robbie was in running shorts (not sure why he owned those because he never ran) and a tee shirt. He had on tennis shoes and a ball cap.

"Are you going out to the clubs?" I asked.

"Dressed like this?" He motioned to his hideous attire. "Baby, you know me." He walked over and gave me a kiss. It made sense what he was saying. Robbie would never go out dressed like that. Robbie always dressed to the nines when he went out. He would wear more gold than Mr. T, I think.

"When will you be back?" I asked.

"Tomorrow. We are just going to drink beer and work on Jack's speed boat way out in the country."

"Okay," I said. I always went into panic mode and gave him the *are you going to cheat or not* look.

He tilted his head slightly and gave a sideways smile. "Baby, it's in the middle of the woods with no bars around."

"Whatever," I replied. Then Dustin walked in, suitcase in hand. "Oh, so Dustin is going too?"

"Yup," Macey said, "but they're taking my car." Macey stood arms crossed. I could tell that Macey was about as happy as I was. The minute they drove off, my stomach dropped.

"Do you think they're telling the truth?" I asked Macey.

"Nope," she replied. That was another long night for me. The last time I talked to Robbie was nine that night, and he didn't answer the phone after that. I stayed awake staring at the ceiling, knowing once again he was screwing around.

It is crazy how much crap you'll put up with when you don't feel you deserve better. I called him I don't know how many times that night and got no answer. I finally fell asleep around four and was up at eight which is not normal for me, especially on a Saturday morning. I slowly walked into the kitchen where Macey was sitting at the bar tapping her fingers like a mad woman.

"I need coffee. I don't want to talk about it till after coffee." Of course, Macey didn't listen to me.

"Dustin never called back after nine."

"I know. Robbie didn't either. I am going to kill him."

We heard her car pulling in, and the anger ran through my body. Robbie and Dustin walked into the house full of grease and super dirty. They both looked exhausted.

"OMG," said Macey. "You both look horrible."

"Sorry, babe," Dustin said. "We worked on that stupid speedboat all night."

Robbie walked up to me and put his arms around me. "I sure missed my baby," he kissed me on top of the head.

"Did not," I replied. "You never answered my calls, all night." I poked my lip out.

"Baby, we were busy working on the boat, and Jack's cordless phone died. It took forever to charge, and I didn't want to wake you up. Do you see how dirty I am? I'm exhausted and need a shower."

I started feeling bad about not trusting him. "I am so sorry," I said. "You are right; you go shower and lie down. I'm going to the grocery store for you and will make you a yummy lunch for when you wake up." Let's be honest, I don't cook but I could make a killer grilled cheese with tater tots.

"Okay," he said and went toward the bedroom. I looked everywhere but I couldn't find Robbie's keys to his truck.

Macey walked in and asked what I was looking for. "I'm trying to find the keys to Robbie's truck to get groceries."

"Let's just take mine," she said.

"Okay, sounds good." I hated putting groceries in the back of Robbie's truck.

The guys were cleaning up, so we left them a note. As we walked around the grocery store, Macey and I talked about how bad we felt for accusing them of doing something they didn't do. "Let's make them a huge dinner," Macey said.

"Yes," I replied. "And dessert."

"Late night dessert too," Macey smiled.

We got a lot of groceries. As we approached the car, Macey popped the trunk. When it opened, the grocery bags fell from my hands to the ground. In the trunk were all the dress clothes that Robbie and Dustin had worn to go out. The trunk reeked of cologne. There was all of Robbie's gold jewelry and empty bags that had white stuff in them. We knew immediately that they had gone out partying.

"I am going to kill him," Macey said and then gritted her teeth like a mad dog.

"No, we are going to leave them." I reached in and grabbed Robbie's oversized clothes. I was so mad. I put on his long-sleeved shirt, his huge jeans, his gold necklace, all his gold rings. Meanwhile Macey was also putting on all of Dustin's clothes.

People passed by and were pointing and laughing at us. I am sure they thought we were crazy, and we were. Crazy pissed-off girlfriends. We threw the groceries in the trunk no more caring about a romantic dinner.

"We should poison them." Macey glared at me.

"That liar! Do you think they just added grease to their clothes?" I asked.

"I'm sure of it," Macey was checking all over the clothes for lipstick, I guess.

When we got to the house, I stormed in. Robbie was passed out. I climbed up on him straddling him like a horse wearing all of his clothes from the trunk. "Open your eyes," I whispered.

He gave a grin like he was about to get some…and he was. When he opened his eyes, they widened in shock. I slapped him across the face. "Wake up!" I knew he was passed out from all the coke he took.

"Look familiar?" I asked. "Look up!" I demanded.

"Baby, please, I can explain."

"No," I replied. "Chin up!" As he lifted his chin, I saw the white around his nose. "I am done," I said.

He tried to pull me close, but I fought him off. "DONE!" I screamed. "AWAY FROM YOU!"

*****

Thank God for Macey's parents. They gave us the money for a deposit on our new apartment downtown. It was really cute, a white Victorian, and looked like something out of the 1920s.

We got settled in, and I thanked God I had a job to help pay the

Fear and Paybacks

rent. Macey and Dustin broke up. That girl was wilder than a stallion horse. She went out almost every night and left me once again all alone.

We lived on the third floor because I refused to live on the ground level. It would be too easy for someone to break in. I felt safe being so high up, but climbing those stairs was not fun. "Top floor is penthouse." Macey would smile. We were far from living a penthouse life, more like a poor house. I didn't care; it was ours.

Not having Robbie's money, we no longer ate like kings; we were living on a budget. We figured out fifty different ways to eat Ramen noodles.

One year, we counted all of our quarters on the floor to get a bottle of wine. Mardi Gras was always fun because we would survive on moon pies and wine.

When I had to stay there by myself, I would never leave the house at night. I was so afraid of the outside world and who was going to hurt me, or take me, or destroy me worse than I already was. Courage was something I didn't know. I locked all the doors and would push big furniture in front of the door. I didn't hide in the closet, but I did hide in my room. Fear paralyzed me once again.

Robbie called me for months, but I wouldn't answer. Work was going great, but I didn't know the big boss had eyes for me. He had secrets, and I was about to be one of them. If only I knew the next man I would fall in love with would be the most dangerous man of all or was he…

I found that I had only started on my path of shame and despair. At this point, I couldn't see what lay ahead and how I would continue living life as a Silent Sinner…

ABOUT THE AUTHOR

JODY PAAR

Jody Paar is from a small town in the south. She was the youngest of three sisters, and her loving mother and father raised her in a happy home.

She was supposed to be a boy but came out all girl. She sparkled from the moment she came into the world. As a little girl, she was always in her mom's makeup and heels. She used her hairbrush to continuously proclaim, "I'll be a star one day."

Jody always lit up a room and never met a stranger, even as a child. She talked with anyone, even if they wouldn't talk to her.

When she became a teenager, she began to rebel, and that continued her on a traumatic rollercoaster life in her early adult years. Jody struggled on a dark path, which only got darker in 2007 when her dad passed away. A year later, her life changed forever when she met her husband Jim Paar. They married in 2009, and her wedding day was the best day of her life.

In 2012, with the help of her husband, Jody started a dream online business she named Soleful Styles that sold bling boots and shoes. But then in 2016, the dream died after experiencing a lot of betrayal when she found herself undercut from her business partner, so she took down her website. Once again, Jody felt defeated, but her husband stuck beside her and helped her launch her next business Bling Life in 2016.

Jody followed in her grandmother's footsteps. Also in 2016, she was crowned Queen of her Mardi Gras group the Mystical Order of Mirams in Orange Beach. She has worked with several charities: Little Pink Houses, The Light House, and Mary's Shelter, to name a few. She has always been about giving back and showing others love.

In 2017, Jody and her husband moved to Nashville, Tennessee. In her opinion, that move was the best decision they had made. One year later after attending the 10X conference, from February 2018 to April 2018, Jody wrote **B.O.S.S. (Break Out Silent Soldier)** and developed the first book in the three-part series.

Jody refuses to allow failure, guilt, or any emotion stop her ever again. Nothing is impossible. The word "Impossible" means "I'm possible." So, to every person who has said, "You Can't," I just proved I can because I did.

So, follow your dreams and never give up!

CPSIA information can be obtained
at www.ICGtesting.com
Printed in the USA
LVOW13s0451260618
581885LV00002BA/3/P